FROM OTHER WISDOM-SEEKERS:

"Kathy, I am so grateful for all your information. You were one of the first 'conscious' people I was guided to in my quest to change my life, and my journey has continued ever since. I could go on and on about the healing that has taken place in my life from Tourette's, heavy narcotics use, multiple prescription drugs, (doctor prescribed), eating gluttonously, and smoking a pack a day, along with just the pressures of growing up in a world like ours. I now KNOW the possibilities are limitless. I thank you for holding the 'bar' so high for conscious eating, living, and loving! I look forward to continuing such a brilliant, promising, and rewarding path alongside people like you."

- Jamison L.

"Kathy, you just can't believe how good I feel now, thanks to you. I love this new life I AM living! Following your wisdom has made it easier for me to love myself and others without any attachments. Thank you for

giving me hope and healing. Thank you for caring and sharing your knowledge. My life is bearable and healthier again, and you have shown me ways to live that I never dreamed were even remotely possible for me. You are an example for me and the entire world. I have so much love and gratitude for you..."

- Beckie S.

"Kathy, I am already finding a HUGE difference in my physical pain levels thanks to some of the shifts I made that you suggested in this program - most of the pain has gone away! I am so grateful. You rock with your knowledge and wisdom. Just thought you needed to KNOW that I appreciate you and your information!"

- Elyn R.

"Thank you, Kathy. I am so inspired by you. Your wisdom is guiding me along my journey to be healthy and make a difference. Without your guidance, I would not be where I am today! I love you."

- Jolene R.

THE POWER OF KNOW

30 DAYS OF ALL-NATURAL WAYS TO HEAL MIND, BODY, AND SPIRIT

WRITTEN BY

KATHY OZZARD CHISM

EDITED BY SUE CRUVER

For Rita ♥
To your Health! ☺
With Love and Gratitude
Kathy ♥

Inquiries should be addressed to Kathy Ozzard Chism, at kathy@kathychism.com

ISBN-13: 9781490484617
ISBN-10: 1490484612

Library of Congress Control Number: 2013912049
CreateSpace Independent Publishing Platform
North Charleston, South Carolina

Printed in the United States of America

First Printing - October 2013

"Mind, body, and spirit are interconnected.
When one suffers, they all suffer.
The master key is to keep all three healthy and joyful...
naturally."

~ Kathy Ozzard Chism

DEDICATION

This book is dedicated to everyone who suffers from Adrenal Burnout Syndrome (ABS) - a stress disease that is affecting millions, yet not currently understood nor recognized by most of the American medical establishment. This book is also dedicated to Jim Reese, a Naturopath and Orthomolecular Nutritionist, who saved my life when I nearly died from stress and ABS in 2009.

INTRODUCTION

I have been curious about health, healing, and the human body ever since age sixteen, when I became a vegetarian.

Since that time, I hungrily devoured (pun intended!) every book I could get my hands on about healthy eating and healthy living, including self-help books for my reoccurring depression. I also wanted to find ways to help my Mother get off eighteen prescription medications she had been taking for a variety of health issues ever since my parents divorced when I was seven years old.

One thing this educational journey taught me is that there is WAY too much conflicting information "out there" about how to be healthy, with more and more coming at us every day.

My guess is that most people get so overwhelmed by it all that they simply give up and just keep doing what they want, eating what they want, and resigning themselves to continuing with the status quo. They ignore or simply accept the current statistics that tell them they will probably succumb at some point to heart disease, cancer, diabetes, or some other debilitating disease.

The more I learned, the more I realized that people need a simple guidebook to start on a healthier, more natural path aligned with who we really are as human beings.

+ A guidebook that takes healing down to basics.

+ A guidebook that makes healthy, all-natural lifestyle changes enticing and easy to follow.

+ A guidebook that simplifies much of the health information out there, turning it into a digestible meal instead of a gargantuan feast.

+ A guidebook that teaches easy ways for taking care of mind, body, and spirit, as all three are equal in importance for homeostasis (the balance of physiological and psychological states).

Perhaps if I had found such a guidebook back in January of 2009 when I nearly died from stress and Adrenal

Burnout Syndrome, I wouldn't have had to go through the subsequent years of pain and hard work to rebuild my various organs that were shutting down.

However, I believe everything happens for a reason. The experience of coming back to life and the wisdom I learned throughout the process inspired me to write a 30-Day program of "Wisdom Snacks"* to help others, as stress and ill-health are so prevalent today.

I launched the program online through my website, www.kathychism.com, with much success. To give even more people the opportunity to change for the better, it made sense to put the knowledge I was giving into book form now instead.

Some "snacks" you will know already... yet we all need reminders from time to time.
Some "snacks" you will resist - these are usually the ones you need the most!
Some "snacks" will be entirely new and eye-opening for you.

All are critical for living at one's optimum level.

No matter how healthy you think you are, I truly believe if you incorporate this program into your daily life, you will be healthier in thirty days than when you started it.

As you embrace and continue to use the "Wisdom Snacks," prepare to be amazed. The longer you follow these suggestions, the healthier you can become.

Over time, they will become second nature, and you will do them with ease. Think of them as thirty gifts you will give yourself.

I gave these gifts to myself, and, along with guided all-natural testing and supplementation from Jim Reese, Naturopath and Orthomolecular Nutritionist, my life was saved.

Yours can be, too.

I honor you for wanting to take this healing journey with me, and for choosing your well-being before anything and anyone else. This is not being selfish - it is simply SELF-ish. Big difference. The more you give to your SELF, the more of yourself you have to give.

Ready? Let's get started!

Here we GROW!

With Love, Health, Peace, Joy, Abundance, and Gratitude,

♥♥♥ *Kathy*

(*Thank you, Stacey Sophia Robyn, for coining and sharing your brilliant "Wisdom Snack" phrase!)

TABLE OF CONTENTS

WISDOM SNACK #1 - BREATH

Let's start with something so basic you may be forgetting about its critical importance throughout your day - breathing!

Think about it. We can go up to ten days without food or water, but only about four minutes without breath. That alone tells us how important it is to B-R-E-A-T-H-E.

KNOW that breathing:

+ expands the spinal column

+ calms the nerves

+ lowers blood pressure

+ improves fat burn and muscle function

✦ provides extra oxygen to the blood, causing the body to release endorphins, which are important for maintaining mental health

Right now, take a few moments to GIVE YOURSELF at least three, slow, deep breaths.

1. in through your <u>nose</u> to the count of four
2. <u>hold</u> to the count of four
3. exhale <u>slowly</u> out through your <u>mouth</u> to the count of eight

NOTE: Instead of sucking in your stomach as you breathe in, which leads to shallow breathing, place one hand on your abdomen over your belly button so you may feel that area expand rather than your chest.

As you inhale, breathe in energy, light, joy, wisdom, bliss, forgiveness, love, acceptance, gratitude, peace, serenity, perfect health, tolerance, creativity, inspiration, clarity, and anything else positive that you would like to attract in and BE in your life.

As you exhale, breath out tension, stress, fear, sadness, lethargy, anger, frustration, resentment, impatience, worry, depression, guilt, grief, trauma, etc. - anything negative you would like to release and not hold anymore.

Then close your eyes and do a scan of your body slowly from head to toe. When you come across any tension, tell it to relax, breathe into it, and then exhale and let it GO.

Do this at least once a day, and ideally, more. Lots more. Put notes all over your home, car, workplace, by your computer, etc., reminding you to do this often every single day.

BREATHE.

Fill your lungs, heart, and mind with the life force.

BREATHE.

So simple.
So powerful.
So healing.

To your expanded, oxygenated health!

♥♥♥ *Kathy*

WISDOM SNACK #2 - WATER

We are water beings. Almost 75% of the human body is water:

+ blood is 83% water

+ muscles are 75% water

+ the brain is 95% water

+ lungs are 90% water

Somewhere along the line, instead of replenishing our cells with pure water daily, many of us started choosing things like sodas (sugar), coffee (acid), alcohol (extremely dehydrating), and other not-so-healthy choices as our main liquid sources.

These choices have taken a terrible toll on the health of millions and millions of people worldwide. Recent studies are finding that even Alzheimer's Disease may be directly related to lack of proper hydration from pure water over time.

The good news is that serious situations like Alzheimer's and many other diseases may be able to be lessened, stopped, and possibly even reversed simply by hydrating our bodies properly with good, pure water!

Drink 4-8 glasses of pure water each day. Drink more when you are in hot weather. Drink pure water before, during, and after exercising. KNOW that if you are thirsty, you are already dehydrated.

Drinking pure water at certain times of the day maximizes its effectiveness on the body. Here are some interesting tips from a cardiac specialist:

1. Two glasses of pure water after waking up - helps activate internal organs.
2. One glass 30 minutes to an hour before a meal - helps digestion. (Try not to drink water with meals, however, as it impedes digestion.)

3. One glass before a bath or hot tub (spa) soak - helps lower blood pressure, and at least one glass after a bath or spa soak replaces fluids.

4. One glass before bed - helps avoid stroke or heart attack.

Here is a tip for replacing electrolytes after exercise. Instead of the commonly used "athlete drink" that contains high fructose corn syrup, citric acid, "natural" flavors, salt, sodium citrate, mono-potassium sulfate, modified food starch, red 40, emulsifiers, and glycerol ester of rosin to provide coloring, switch to a product like "Essentia Water."

Not only does Essentia Water hydrate better and replace electrolytes without all of that nasty stuff in it, it also has a pH of 9.5. This means it helps turn your body more alkaline, which is awesome. (More on the critical importance of pH and alkalinity in a later Wisdom Snack.)

I first learned about Essentia Water when I was struck with food poisoning. Feeling absolutely horrible, I called my Naturopath, who said to start drinking Essentia Water immediately, which I did. Unlike other times with food poisoning when it took two to three days to feel normal again, I was fine and back to work in only three hours! Amazing.

Now I keep it in my cupboard at all times. I start every morning with it, drink it whenever I feel a bit "off," and have found it to be great for relieving headaches as well. You may find it online and at most health food stores, and can usually save money if you purchase it by the case. Although I am not a fan of plastic bottles, at least theirs are BPA-free and recyclable.

Please also consider installing a reverse osmosis system at home for your tap water for drinking, washing vegetables, etc. If you can afford it, get a salt soft water system for your entire home as well, as the water you shower, bathe, and brush your teeth in has potentially harmful chemicals that enter your body and blood stream. The more these chemicals can be removed ahead of time, the better.

There are also water filter faucet attachments that will remove some harmful chemicals. It is worth getting any good filtration system you can to help reduce the continued toxic load on the body.

One more thing. If you do drink alcohol, please be sure to drink an 8 oz. glass of water <u>before</u> AND another

<u>after</u> every glass of alcohol, as alcohol is <u>extremely</u> dehydrating. You will have far fewer hangovers, too.

If you have not been drinking enough water daily, when you add more to your routine you may notice a brief period of water weight gain. That's OK. The reason is that your body has learned to hoard water when it receives it, since it never knows when it is going to get it again.

Once your body understands that you are now going to hydrate daily, it will stop the hoarding, and you will lose that extra little bit of weight.

Over time, prepare to be amazed at how much better you feel simply because you are hydrating properly, especially as water is a major key for flushing toxins from the body. (More on toxins in a later Wisdom Snack, too.)

I am now at a point where my only drinks are pure water, green juices, and a rare glass of red wine on special occasions... and that's it. When your body starts getting what it really wants and needs, it no longer craves what it truly doesn't want and need.

Ditch the unhealthy choices and drink pure water instead. Watch healing <u>really</u> happen. As they say, instead of medication, choose more hydration...

To your flow of health, dear Water Being!

♥♥♥ *Kathy*

WISDOM SNACK #3 - STRESS

"Stress Kills." I heard that throughout my life, and knew it vaguely to be true. However, it wasn't until I nearly died in early 2009 that I truly "got it."

My adrenals, thyroid, gall bladder, and ability to assimilate any nutrients from foods had all shut down. My endocrine (hormone) system was also completely haywire... and the root cause of all this? STRESS.

Yes, little Miss Healthy Eater since age sixteen and Advocate For Healthy Living - me - nearly died. How could this happen? Well...

I was taking on way too much in my work life, kept saying "yes" to requests I should have said "no" to, and wasn't getting enough sleep to do it all. Even worse, for two straight years I had an ongoing, seemingly end-less, daily crisis situation going on in my life behind the scenes that was stressful beyond words.

Any of that sound familiar?!

This is something critical to KNOW. When we are under stress, only cortisol and adrenaline are produced - the "fight or flight" hormones. The 39+ other hormones that need to be produced in our bodies on a daily basis are not manufactured when these two show up. Not good.

Our dear bodies try to compensate for the lack of hor-monal nutrients for as long as they can, and then they simply have to give up. Each person is different. I was told that had I not been a vegetarian most of my life, a non-smoker, and someone who rarely drank alcohol, I would have gone into the danger zone far sooner than I did.

It is VITAL that we all manage our stress levels, no mat-ter what is going on, or otherwise we can die. Take my word for it... and no problem is worth that!

Although I agree proper vitamin supplements are of-ten important, (always work with a Naturopath who can test you so you are not choosing supplements or amounts that might actually be harmful for you), the more vitamins and nutrients we can get organically from Nature, the better.

Along with deep breathing properly and often, (very stress reducing), and drinking proper amounts of pure water and organic green veggie juices to flush stress-producing toxins out of your body, here is another of my many all-natural, stress-reducing suggestions:

Eat 6-10 raw, organic almonds per day. Be sure to soak them in pure water for an hour or so. Then, remove the skins and eat them immediately. (Don't store them, even in a refrigerator.) Almonds have magnesium, calcium, B vitamins, and vitamin E - all super important for reducing the effects of stress.

The reason you want to soak the almonds is because the outer brown covering is difficult to digest. Place a desired amount in a bowl, cover the almonds with pure water, and place a breathable fabric or mesh over the bowl for an hour or two. This soaking also ignites the "life force" within the almonds, and "live" foods are always more desirable than non-live foods.

Remember, everything in moderation, including almonds. Try not to eat more than one ounce of almonds per day. Although fabulous for protein, vitamins, and reducing stress in small doses like this, too many may cause lethargy, blurred vision, headaches, diarrhea, and flatulence... and the manganese in them could interfere with certain over-the-counter and prescribed medications.

(Of course, the whole point of this book is to get so healthy you never need medications - of any kind! Yes, this can happen. I haven't even taken an aspirin since 2009.)

As you journey through the thirty Wisdom Snacks in this program, you will learn many more of the incredibly easy, yet powerful, all-natural ways for healing and handling stress that brought me back to life. They will help bring you back to life, too, if you do them.

Just as the quote says at the beginning of this book, KNOW that your mind, body, and spirit are interconnected. When one suffers, they all suffer. Keep all three healthy and joyful, for when you do, stress will no longer be your enemy.

View your stresses as reminders. Do what you need to do to keep mind, body, and spirit in balance, no matter how intense the stresses may be.

To your calm and peaceful health!

♥♥♥ Kathy

WISDOM SNACK #4 - WALKING

KNOW that human beings are meant to walk. Early humans were nomads in a constant search for food and water - walking, walking, walking... and using their "fight or flight" hormones only for fight or flight.

Our bodies love walking.

Walking:

+ reduces the risk of heart disease, cancer, diabetes, and high blood pressure

+ removes toxins through the lymphatic system, which is critical for good health

+ helps control weight

+ strengthens muscles and bones

✦ can decrease your risk of developing osteoporosis
   and arthritis

For those under stress, more vigorous exercise can actually do more damage than good to your adrenals and
thyroid. However, walking is still beneficial for the reasons listed above.

In addition, slowing down, breathing deeply, and connecting with Nature as you walk will feed your soul. Notice
the beauty of everything around you, even if at first glance
you may not think where you are walking is beautiful.

Really look at the trunks, leaves, and branches of trees,
notice the feel of the air on your face, the energy of the
sun or rain, the force of life in weeds growing through
cracks in a sidewalk, the colors surrounding you, (or the
beauty of the monotone shades you see), and the marvel-
ous creation of any creatures you encounter along your
way, be they insect, feathered, reptilian, furry, or human.

Always try to distance yourself as you walk from the
toxins of car exhausts, cigarette smoke, manufacturing
plant discharges, etc. If it is not fresh, clean air, try to get
as far away from it as possible.

Even if you hate to exercise, walk. Try to walk at least two miles daily. If you need some nudges, try these:

+ Park your car much further away than you normally would from a store or your work and walk to the door.

+ Get up from the computer regularly and walk around your office or house.

+ Choose a time every day that you are going to use for your walk. Stick to it.

+ Get a walking speedometer and/or odometer to see how fast and how far you are walking. Set some goals. You don't have to start with two miles the first day. Do what is comfortable for you, and work up to at least that. The odometer will be very motivating.

+ Encourage friends, family, or co-workers to walk with you.

+ Visit an art gallery and walk every floor. Twice.

+ Adopt a rescue dog and walk him/her daily - giving you both a new lease (leash?!) on life.

+ Once you are in a rhythm of walking daily, join or create a walk for charity.

The more people walk, the more support we can raise for the creation of additional walkable places. We will also decrease air pollution, traffic congestion, and reduce health care needs and costs. It's all GOOD.

One more thing. Due to physical limitations, some people are not able to walk right now, or perhaps long term. Consider choosing to take people in either situation for "walks" regularly by pushing their wheelchairs so they, too, may experience the beauty of Nature more often in their area.

You may also want to suggest this book to them. Many positive healing experiences from seemingly impossible situations have occurred when the all-natural wisdom from all thirty snacks is utilized regularly.

OK, finish reading this "snack," and then get up and go for a WALK. :)

To your healthy forward strides!

♥♥♥ Kathy

WISDOM SNACK #5 - F.L.A.G

In January of 2005, thanks to a number of wonderful people and an amazing set of circumstances, I created an all-volunteer nonprofit called Dream One World.

One day I was playing around with ideas for a flag to represent the organization, when I was suddenly struck with the thought that the letters in "flag" stand for:

+ Forgiveness

+ Love

+ Acceptance

+ Gratitude

Taking it a step further, my heart realized that these four words had to apply to <u>everyone</u> - ourselves and ALL others - no exceptions.

In speaking this acronym to my dear friend Helene Barbara, she commented that the four words also had to be for "what is." I instantly agreed.

From that moment on, my life has never been the same.

Was it easy for me to switch into this thought patterning? No.

Has it become easier and more natural over time? Yes.

Am I perfect with using it? Not yet.

Do I still catch myself in old patterns of upset? Yes - yet less and less, and when I see myself going there, I can usually make the change quickly.

KNOW this F.L.A.G. acronym is so HUGE, that if you grasp it and use it 24/7, simple amazing shifts can happen. Your health can improve, and your life can begin flowing in directions you never dreamed possible.

Let me show you how.

FORGIVENESS
Imagine forgiving yourself for everything you have ever done and said in your life. Imagine forgiving all others, no matter what they have done to you, to others, and to our planet. Imagine forgiving what is, instead of fighting it.

LOVE
Next, imagine loving yourself unconditionally. Imagine loving all others, no exceptions, unconditionally. Imagine loving "what is" unconditionally, even if "what is" feels or looks terrible to you right now.

ACCEPTANCE
Now, imagine accepting yourself for who you are. Imagine accepting all others, no exceptions, for who they are or were. Imagine accepting "what is," no matter what.

GRATITUDE
Then, imagine being grateful for being YOU. Imagine being grateful for all others in your life, all on the planet now, and all those who have come before us. Imagine being grateful for "what is."

Now, imagine if everyone did this.

As my sister-in-love Stacey Sophia Robyn, the Goddess of Gratitude, says, "Holy Wow." (Be sure to do Stacey's

"Go Gratitude Experiment" at www.gogratitude.com - it will help transform your life for the better in beautiful ways.)

Please understand this never means you condone hurtful and harmful behaviors. What truly flying your F.L.A.G. means is to let go of your attachment to any of them, and BE healthy.

You focus instead on living in a much higher vibration of love, peace, kindness, health, bliss, and joy. You create solutions and healthy alternatives instead of continually stirring the pot of blame, anger, hatred, jealousy, regret, bitterness, envy, and feeling victimized.

What you begin to understand is that we truly are all ONE. When we hurt another, we hurt ourselves. When we hurt ourselves, we hurt all others. When we continue the flow of upset in the world, we are part of the problem instead of being part of the solution.

In traditional Chinese medicine, which has been practiced for more than 5,000 years, the liver and gallbladder are associated with anger. The heart and small intestine are associated with joy (or lack thereof). The spleen and stomach are associated with over-thinking or pensiveness. The lungs and large intestine are associated with grief. The kidneys and bladder are associated with fear.

Many illnesses "miraculously" disappear once negative emotions are released.

Mind/Body/Spirit - remember, your job is to keep all three as happy and healthy as possible every single day. Do your job well, and you will BE well.

Keep coming from your heart, speak your truths to all in a kind and loving manner, and fly your F.L.A.G. always and in all ways. Watch miracles happen.

To your FLAG-waving healthy self!

♥♥♥

WISDOM SNACK #6 -
pH AND ALKALINITY

Greetings again, Wisdom Seeker! I am happy you are continuing forward on your path to optimal health for mind, body, and spirit... and so proud of you for caring enough about yourself and your family to do so.

Today's Wisdom Snack is a little science lesson.

I would venture to say that the vast majority of people on the planet do not understand or even KNOW how critically important pH and Alkalinity are for their health. I didn't. Once I learned about this, I was amazed at the positive directions my life took and continues to take simply by changing to a more alkaline diet.

Our bodies do not want to be acidic in the fluids or tissues. If they are, all sorts of problems can occur, making the body readily available for disease.

A healthy body has alkaline reserves to neutralize acids. Yet with today's societal eating/drinking habits, and/or coupled with stressful living, these reserves are often depleted or used up... and the body becomes weak in many areas.

Like everything else in life, you want to be in BALANCE.

The good news is that you CAN restore and maintain a balanced body. There is a very easy scientific test with a pH and Alkalinity testing tape you may use in the privacy of your own home to see how you are progressing. You may find these testing strips online, (Micro Essential Lab carries a great Hydrion saliva and urine pH paper), or at most health food stores.

Much of the information below is from the American Journal of Clinical Nutrition:

URINE pH

Test your first urine of the day. Place the tape in the stream, shake it off, and immediately compare it to the chart. If it is at 7.0, perfect. If above that number, you are a little alkaline. If below that number, you are acidic, and you are in trouble.

Do everything you can to do get that number back up to 7.0, like eating your organic green veggies, which want to be 75% of every meal, and drinking Essentia Water. *(Go easy on the spinach, kale, and chard though, as the oxalic acid in these three may interfere with the absorption of magnesium, iron, sodium, and potassium, and has been linked to the formation of kidney stones. A suggestion is to choose one of these once a week.)*

The results of urine testing indicate how well your body is assimilating minerals - especially calcium, magnesium, sodium, and potassium. These are called the "acid buffers," because they are used by the body to control the acid level. If acid levels are too high, the body will not be able to excrete acid. It must either store the acid in body tissues (autotoxication) or buffer it - that is, borrow minerals from organs, bones, etc., in order to neutralize acidity.

SALIVA pH

You will also want to test the pH of your saliva. **Never stick a test strip in your mouth!** Put some saliva on a spoon, and dip the test strip into that.

The results of saliva testing indicate the activity of digestive enzymes in your body, especially the activity of the liver and the stomach. This reveals the flow of enzymes running through your body, and shows their effect on all the body systems. Some people will have acidic pH readings from both urine and saliva. This is referred to as "double acid."

There are many schools of thought about what foods are acidic, and what foods are alkaline. Many are obviously acidic - like coffee, vinegars, tomatoes, citrus, etc. Others might surprise you - like beans, meat, dairy, most nuts (except almonds), corn, white potatoes, canned fruits, all fruit juices, and all sugars.

Some people might tell you that items like tomatoes and lemons in water actually turn to alkaline ash once in your system. This is not true. Acids going into your mouth and then into your stomach to react with hydrochloric acid do not magically become alkaline. It is scientifically impossible.

Many will tell you the benefits of drinking coffee. KNOW that any possible benefits of coffee are overridden by its high acid-producing qualities. Please, view coffee as a poison, and eliminate it as soon as possible from your life.

Please also see the non-organic 5-Hour Energy Drinks on the market as poisons, too. They mess with the endocrine system big time, having the same negative effects of sugar highs, and help create acidity in the body from the caffeine. Thirteen deaths in 2012 were attributed directly to energy drinks for a variety of reasons, including too much B-12. The human body is a system... too much of any good thing can, and usually does, create a bad thing for it.

Your body can only assimilate nutrients and minerals properly if your pH is balanced. If it is too acidic, any nutrients or supplements you take in may not be easily absorbed.

Again, from the American Journal of Clinical Nutrition:

"The reason acidosis is more common in our society is mostly due to the Standard American Diet, ('SAD'), which is far too high in acid-producing animal products like meat, eggs, and dairy, and far too low in alkaline-producing foods like organic fresh vegetables.

Additionally, we eat acid-producing processed foods like white flour and sugar, and drink acid-producing beverages like coffee and soft drinks. We use too many drugs, which are acid forming, and we use artificial chemical sweeteners like NutraSweet, Equal, or aspartame, which are extremely acid-forming and dangerous. One of the best things we can do to correct an overly acidic body is to clean up our diets and lifestyles.

Acidity forces the body to borrow minerals - including calcium, sodium, potassium, and magnesium - from vital organs and bones to buffer (neutralize) the acid, and safely remove it from the body. Because of this strain, the body can suffer severe and prolonged damage due to high acidity - a condition that can go undetected for years.

Mild acidosis can cause such problems as:

+ Cardiovascular damage, including the constriction of blood vessels and the reduction of oxygen

+ Weight gain, obesity, and diabetes

+ Immune deficiency

+ Acceleration of free radical damage, possibly contributing to cancerous mutations

+ Premature aging

+ Osteoporosis; weak, brittle bones, hip fractures, and bone spurs

✦ Joint pain, aching muscles, and lactic acid buildup

✦ Low energy and chronic fatigue

A recent seven-year study conducted on 9,000 women at the University of California, San Francisco, showed that those who have chronic acidosis are at greater risk for bone loss that those who have normal pH levels. The scientists who carried out this experiment believe that many of the hip fractures prevalent among middle-aged women are connected to high acidity caused by a diet rich in animal foods and low in vegetables. This is because the body borrows calcium from the bones in order to balance pH."

Your pH and alkalinity throughout life is HUGE. Pay close attention to it, and it will help guide you to a far healthier, and, most probably, longer life.

To your balanced, alkaline well-being!

♥♥♥ Kathy

WISDOM SNACK #7 - NATURE

"Our bodies are our gardens - our wills are our gardeners."
- William Shakespeare

+ Are you tending to your garden?

+ Are you giving it healthy, organic, plant-based foods and clean, pure water?

+ Are you giving it rest, relaxation, sunshine, exercise, and fun time?

+ Are you pushing it to its limits and asking it to go beyond its capacity?

+ Are you stressing it to the point of breakdown and plague?

How you tend to your garden - your magnificent body, mind, and spirit - determines every aspect of your life.

Tend wisely, and KNOW that it is our nature to be in Nature.

As more and more of us live and work indoors, we lose our connection to the earth, the sky, the sun, the moon, the stars, the trees, the flowers, and even fresh air.

We have distanced ourselves from the nurturing, healthy, organic foods and pure water we were always meant to take in in to keep our bodies running smoothly and supported.

We live frenetic, "I'm too busy" lives, where most of us rarely recharge our own batteries by slowing down and uniting with Source and Mother Earth... and then we wonder why we are feeling so lost, unhealthy, and disconnected.

+ Fifteen minutes of sun per day on your pineal gland (third eye, forehead) produces a healthy daily dose of Vitamin D.

+ Thalassotherapy (exposure to sea air and immersion in warm sea water, mud, clay, and protein-rich algae) helps restore the body's natural chemical balance.

+ Walking barefoot on the earth connects you to the subtle, yet ever-present energy on the earth's surface and below, grounding you to a deep sense of well-being.

STOP! Take a break from your "to-do" list!

Although I tend to be a bit of a workaholic, one day before moving away from northern California, I took my own advice, and dropped everything to go to the beach. Forty-five minutes later, I was witnessing a very rare whale pod, seals, birds, and a gorgeous sunset. I left feeling on top of the world.

No matter where you live or how busy you are, there is beauty all around you just waiting to fill your soul and lift your spirits. Just as we were meant to be ONE with each other, we are meant to be ONE with our planet and all its gifts. GO! Look for them! You have permission! ☺

"I only went out for a walk,
and finally concluded to stay out till sundown,
for going out, I found, was really going in."
- John Muir

BE who you were truly meant to be... a child of Nature. Put down the cell phone, get up from the computer, walk away from the TV... and go outside.

Hug a tree. Go barefoot. Gaze up at the sky. Shut your eyes. Feel the breeze, the warmth of the sun. Visit a stream, a river, a lake, or the ocean, and feel the water. Connect to our Earth today... and every day. Enjoy, in JOY!

In doing so, like all of Nature, YOU will grow and flourish.

To your all-natural health...

♥♥♥ *Kathy*

WISDOM SNACK #8 -
"YES" AND "NO"

"Everything you say yes to
means you are saying no to something else.
Are you saying yes to the right things?"
- Melanie Benson Strick

Many of my clients first come to me in complete over-whelm. At the time, they are saying "yes" to way too much, and "no" to very little.

They feel that if they don't do the tasks before them, no one will... or certainly not as well as they could. I point out that if they die from stress, someone else will do those tasks anyway.

KNOW the key is to choose things you LOVE to do that bring you joy and prosperity, and let GO of those things you love less. In this case, less really IS more.

I worked with a client recently who is so helpful to everyone else at her job she forgets to help herself. As a result, she becomes exhausted, stressed, and overwhelmed. I told her she has permission to create boundaries with others, and suggested she speak her needs about needing to finish one task before taking on the next to those who ask her to drop everything and help them right NOW. She took my advice, and is feeling far less stressed at work.

Setting boundaries and taking care of YOU is critical. This creates health in mind, body, spirit, and relationships.

I had to learn this lesson the hard way by nearly dying. I learned that trying to do it ALL is not really my purpose. Instead, simply doing the best I can, when I can, however I can, and letting go of any expectations is my true calling.

The interesting thing is that once I shifted to that mindset, doors I never even knew existed started opening, and far more joy was brought in without me having to do all the work! Make the shift, and the same can be true for YOU, too.

Stop a minute. Breathe. Take an inventory of your life. Are you doing too much? Saying "Yes" to too much? What can you eliminate to make your life more manageable, more sane, more joyful?

Do it! Remember, you give more of yourself when you have more of your SELF to give.

Right now, take a moment to give yourself three deep breaths. Close your eyes and do a scan of your body slowly from head to toe. When you come across any tension, tell it to relax, and let it GO.

When you feel centered in your heart, ask yourself these questions, and be open to the thoughts that appear as answers:

+ Who am I?

+ What do I want to do with my life?

+ Where do I want to be living?

+ When will I be ready to be who I really am?

+ With whom do I want to share my life?

+ How will my dreams come true?

+ What is my purpose?

As you ask yourself these questions, just let whatever bubbles up be there and look at it objectively. There are no right or wrong answers, just the inner YOU lighting your path.

What I have found in my own life and in the lives of so many of my friends, family members, and clients, is that we keep putting the needs of others before our own.

We have difficulty saying "no" to family, to friends, to our employers and co-workers... even to our pets when they ask for something! We are always serving others, yet not taking the necessary time to give to ourselves.

Imagine if we drove our cars without ever putting gas in them. It wouldn't be long before they died on the street. Imagine how long our digital cameras and cell phones would work without recharging the batteries.

Why do we think our bodies, minds, and spirits can just go and go and go without any recharging?!

"STOP IT!" After I learned to say this to myself, I started saying it to my overworked and overstressed clients.

At first they are stunned, and then they always giggle. These two simple words bring people back to their senses. They begin to see that if they can make the shift to take more time for themselves, they can climb out of the quicksand pulling them down, down, down... and choose a lighter, brighter, more joyful way to live.

Here is something else I love to say to my clients, while waving a pretend magic wand in the air: "You now have permission to speak your truth kindly to everyone and not take on anything that does not feel right to you. Only do what you can do, and nothing more."

Many tear up at this one, too afraid to grant this to themselves. It is as if they need permission from someone else to say "no." When asked, they immediately say it is OK for everyone else to take time off, just not them.

Dear One, it is time to shift that perception. As we get busier and busier, trying to do it all, we get sicker and sicker individually and as a nation - have you noticed?

Let's all return to a place of peace and sanity, and to good health and loving relationships. Learning to say "no" to what doesn't support your highest good, and "yes" to what does, is part of that.

As Helene Barbara said about this Wisdom Snack, "Go from 'Yes' and 'No' to 'Yes' and 'KNOW.' "

"For peace of mind,
resign as general manager of the universe."
- Author Unknown

Oh, and trying to be who you think others want you to be only leads to frustration and suppression of the soul.

BE who you really are, regardless of what others think. Living from your heart and speaking your truth opens your world and allows your spirit to soar.

To your truthful and more relaxed self!

♥♥♥ *Kathy*

WISDOM SNACK #9 - SIMPLIFY

"Simplify to simply fly."
- Kathy Ozzard Chism

The above quote came to me many years ago, and ever since I have felt the power of these words grow ever stronger.

KNOW that clutter stops energy from flowing. It creates chaos, both physically and emotionally.

+ Is your home, car, and/or desk usually a mess?

+ Do you find you often can't remember where you put things?

+ Is your mind so full of "stuff" each day that you feel completely frazzled?

✦ Do you spend more time than you should looking for things in drawers, cabinets, and/or closets?

✦ Are your important papers scattered around your desk or home instead of in easy-to-access files?

✦ Do you ever bounce checks or are late on payments due to not being organized?

✦ Are you often late to appointments and events?

✦ Do you always feel like you are rushed?

✦ Do you often come out of stores with more than you intended to buy when you went in?

Answering "yes" to any of the questions above signifies it is time for you to organize, (de-clutter, create files, make lists, keep a calendar, etc.), and simplify.

Life is not about the stuff. If nothing else, the financial "crash" in 2008 and subsequent recession has been proof of that fact. Life is about relationships, peace of mind, joy, health, purpose, love, etc.

A friend told me she is so overwhelmed by the clutter in her home she doesn't have the energy to clean it up. My advice was to start small, say one drawer in her bedroom, and have the satisfaction of sorting it out. Next day, clean another drawer, or maybe two. Next day, do the top of her end table.

Stay focused on one room at a time, and before you know it, you will have at least one place of peace in your home. Give yourself a little healthy reward each time you complete a room.

Keep going, day by day, room by room, and soon your home will become a true sanctuary again. Donate or sell items you no longer need and feel good about others having the opportunity to use them.

When you have many items, hold a garage sale for yourself or for charity. My book, "Garage Sale Success Secrets," gives you step-by-step guidelines for creating highly successful sales, and Zen-like tips for creating a happier life in the process.

For an eye-opening look at all our consumptive patterns to spur you on, go on You Tube and find the clever and educational video called "The Story of Stuff," with the engaging Annie Leonard.

Remember, you must always create space for what you want in life.

If your closet is full, there is no more room for a new article of clothing. Something must go.

If you want a quality relationship, hanging on to an unfulfilling relationship does not create the space for the right person to appear.

If you want a new job or career, staying somewhere that makes you miserable does not create the space for a new opportunity.

If you keep your heart closed, you are not creating space for love and divine guidance to enter.

Simplify, open up, create space, and receive with gratitude.

To your calmer, more organized, and productive self!

♥♥♥ Kathy

WISDOM SNACK #10 - HAPPINESS

*"Happiness is a matter of opinion -
life's good if you think it's good
and bad if you think it's bad."*
- Steve Fowler

✦ If you always see yourself as a victim, you will always feel victimized.

✦ If you always see yourself as poor, you will always feel poor.

✦ If you always see yourself as unhealthy, you will always feel unhealthy.

✦ If you always see yourself as ugly, you will always feel ugly.

✦ If you always see yourself as burdened, you will always feel burdened.

Starting to see a pattern here? Now, what if these shift to...

+ If you always see yourself as strong, you will always feel strong.

+ If you always see yourself as abundant, you will always feel abundant.

+ If you always see yourself as healthy, you will always feel healthy.

+ If you always see yourself as beautiful, you will always feel beautiful.

+ If you always see yourself as as light and free, you will always feel light and free.

OK, maybe the word "always" is a little too absolute, but you get what I mean!

KNOW that how you see yourself has a LOT to do with the health of your mind, body, spirit, and even finances. There are ALWAYS (here I will use that word as an absolute) things to be grateful for, no matter how horrible something might be.

I hear this from my friend Edward, who spent twenty years on death row in Uganda for a crime he didn't commit, from my friend Danny who was paralyzed from the neck down when a truck coming out of a one-way street the wrong way hit him, from friends who have lost their children, their homes, their eyesight... you name it.

Stay in gratitude for what you have, not in despair for what you don't have. Gratitude actually releases positive endorphins! Think of at least five things every day that you are grateful for... and to really raise your gratitude levels, do the Go Gratitude Experiment at www.gogratitude.com.

"When I am anxious it is because I am living in the future. When I am depressed it is because I am living in the past."
- Author Unknown

I love this quote. It says it all about living in the NOW, as that is all there really is. So much DIS-ease that can lead to disease can be avoided if people simply stay present in the present, and embrace it with an open heart.

What was, was.

What will be, will be.

By fully experiencing every moment and staying in the NOW, no matter how difficult at times it may be, you are truly living, learning, and growing stronger!

Focus on who YOU really are - a kind, intelligent, loving, caring, creative, fun, beautiful soul - instead of envying someone else's talents or money or relationships or looks or whatever.

BE who you REALLY are, not merely a sliver of potential.

BE happy.

To your empowered radiant health!

♥♥♥ *Kathy*

NOTE: When you are feeling sorry for yourself, KNOW that this is a great time to help someone else less fortunate. It's a win-win for you and the recipient. Sharing love and kindness is like taking a happy pill for YOU while you help heal the world. Donate to a charity, volunteer your time to help some children in need, perform a random act of kindness, adopt a rescue animal, give that senior person your seat on the bus, whatever... focus on others, and your world will only get brighter.

WISDOM SNACK #11 - HEALING TOUCH

"Touching is nourishment."
- Gay Luce

What is the first sense we connect with as we enter the world? Touch.

What is the first thing you do when you bump into something and hurt yourself? Rub it.

What is our natural instinct to do when someone is crying? Hug them. (Did you also KNOW that hugs can actually lower the risk of heart disease?!)

We are meant to touch each other <u>often</u> in safe, nurturing ways... from the moment of birth through our very last breath.

The effects of touch deprivation, as well as inappropriate touch, are staggering in our society. Both cause depression, anger, (often leading to violence and abuse), increased illness, etc.

More and more of us are living alone, too... adding to the touch deprivation that is rampant in today's world. Want an easy cure? Therapeutic Massage!

Below is a bullet list of 35 incredibly important massage benefits for mind, body, and spirit. Massage assists <u>every single system</u> of the body, and helps each to function better.

Sadly, most people consider massage a "luxury," and yet will think nothing of spending hundreds to thousands of dollars each year on pharmaceutical medications, alcohol, shopping sprees, or whatever else they can think of to make them "feel better." Ironically, these things can often make them feel worse.

Look at how much better off they would be getting a massage:

✦ Physically relaxes the body

✦ Calms the nervous system

✦ Lowers blood pressure

✦ Reduces heart rate

✦ Slows respiration

✦ Loosens tight muscles

✦ Stretches connective tissues

✦ Reduces chronic pain

✦ Improves skin tone

✦ Increases blood and lymph circulation

✦ Speeds the removal of metabolic waste

✦ Increases red blood cell counts

✦ Relieves tired and aching muscles

✦ Stimulates the release of endorphins

✦ Improves muscle tone

✦ Relieves cramps and muscle spasms

✦ Increases flexibility and range of motion

✦ Promotes deeper and more effective breathing

✦ Speeds recovery from injuries and illness

✦ Strengthens the immune system

✦ Reduces swelling

✦ Reduces scarring

✦ Improves posture

✦ Reduces tension headaches

✦ Increases tissue metabolism

✦ Decreases muscular deterioration

MENTAL BENEFITS OF MASSAGE THERAPY:

✦ Reduces mental stress

✦ Promotes better sleep

✦ Calms a bad temper

✦ Induces mental relaxation

✦ Improves concentration

EMOTIONAL BENEFITS OF MASSAGE THERAPY

+ Reduces anxiety

+ Enhances self-image

+ Provides a feeling of well-being

+ Promotes greater creative expression

*(Many thanks to Night Owl Press for much of the above information.)

In my perfect world, everyone on the planet would get a massage once a week! Imagine - all of humanity would be so much happier and healthier.

For YOU, get massages as often as you can. Find a qualified therapist. In America, a great place to start is through the American Massage Therapy Association at www.amtamassage.org.

Ideally, you want the therapist to use Biotone Organic Pure Touch massage gel, (I bring my own for them to use), or a similar organic product, as anything that goes on your skin will end up in your bloodstream in minutes and be distributed throughout your body. Pure Touch is the cleanest massage gel I have found to date.

Touch and hearing are the last two senses humans experience in life. If someone is dying and you can be with them as they are passing, speak love into their ears. Gently lay your hand on a shoulder, in their hand, over their heart, or wherever you feel guided, to let them know you are there and they are not alone.

When it is our time, may all of us KNOW we are deeply loved as we cross over. Gentle touch is a profound way to convey that. If you cannot be there in person, send energy from your heart to theirs. They will feel it, as we are all energy beings, and intent is powerful.

Now, go give someone a hug. Make sure they hug you back. Go get a therapeutic massage, too.

To your touching, loving, happier, healthier self!

 Kathy

WISDOM SNACK #12 - SUN AND LIGHT

We humans are meant to be in the sun.

Please be sure to get at least 15 - 30 minutes of sun every day on your pineal gland area (forehead - the "third eye" location) to produce necessary Vitamin D for your body. On non-sunny days, I suggest taking Vitamin D supplements to maintain your Vitamin D levels... and if you work mainly indoors, you may want to take these supplements daily. (I favor the ones from Pro Caps Labs.) Again, it is always best to check with a Naturopath to test for the amount you need.

Please try NOT to use sunscreen. If we were meant to be covered up and out of the sun all the time, we would have been born with thick fur and live underground like moles, right?! ☺

I have felt for many, many years that the sun wasn't the issue around skin cancer, but rather all the goo we put on our bodies - lotions, sunscreens, non-organic make-up, etc. - and now there is the science to back that up.

When you use sunscreen, you are covering your skin with chemicals that get absorbed quickly into the blood-stream. Some of these can actually promote cancer. KNOW the skin needs vitamin D, which helps prevent skin cancer.

Of course, there will be times when you need to do something to prevent burning, so when you feel the need to use sunscreen, be sure to read the ingredients and choose something organic and as healthy as possible.

As we make a conscious effort to stop putting chemicals in and on our bodies, we will be healthier for it.

KNOW about LIGHT, too:

> "Light is the purest healing force in the universe. Plenty of full spectrum light each day equals good health and lots of energy. Light and air are primary

sources of vital energy, and create a strong immune system.

We need a balance of all the spectrum colors, and we pick them up through our eyes and skin. Most of us spend 90% of our life indoors. Ideally, you should be exposed to at least 30 minutes of full spectrum light every day.

If we are in an environment which offers little opportunity for natural light and air, we operate at half our premium level. Our brain may be dull and fuzzy, we may have poor memory, or find it hard to think clearly or make decisions.

Emotionally we feel drained and depressed without knowing why. Physically we may suffer from fatigue and recurrent viral or bacterial infections. Natural light also influences our pituitary gland and pineal gland, which control and normalize the release of hormones into the body that are closely linked with mood and emotions.

Our home or office environments can greatly influence our ability to absorb vital energy into our system, and so directly affect our well-being and quality of life. It is essential we pay attention to the *light and air in our home if we are to improve our health and lifestyle."*

(From "The Healing Home," by Suzy Chiazzari)

Now, please do not use those swirly "CFL" light bulbs. Ever.

Any fluorescent bulb plays havoc with the nervous system, and those bulbs also contain mercury. If one is dropped and broken, well, the EPA has a whole <u>page</u> filled with alarming directions about what to do for adults, children, pets... including leaving the home immediately, opening windows, shutting down heating or air conditioning systems, etc. Yikes!

My guess is not everyone is disposing of these bulbs properly as well, so mercury toxins are going into our landfills, our earth, our water supply, etc. Not good.

Years ago, I had "Solatubes" installed throughout my home. They are AMAZING. No heat, no fading of upholstery, artwork, or rugs, no bugs, no leaking - simply pure, beautiful, natural sunlight that is captured through a patented system streaming into rooms every day. (They can be electrified, too, for nighttime.)

I used to have SAD syndrome, (Seasonal Affective Disorder), but it disappeared once the Solatubes were installed. Plus the savings from not using light bulbs during the day is incredible, and I love that they do so much to help the environment.

There are new LED light bulbs available now, too, that are relatively cool to the touch, use very little electricity, save you money, last for many, many years, and are far safer and healthier for both you and the environment. I installed some of those as well, and they are fantastic. Some are dimmable. As of this writing, there are no 3-way LED bulbs yet, but as regular or dimming bulbs, they are wonderful.

Lighten your world, lighten your life.

To your healthy, light, and sunny self!

 Kathy

WISDOM SNACK #13 - SUGAR

Remember I mentioned at the beginning of this book that the Wisdom Snacks you resist the most are usually the ones you need the most?!

This Wisdom Snack on sugar tends to get a LOT of resistance. Yet, the Wisdom Seekers who make the following vitally important diet change receive health benefits throughout life that are often nothing short of amazing. Please read every word below.

KNOW that refined sugars added to foods and drinks are your #1 enemy for optimal health and weight.

Even so-called "healthy" foods and drinks may have sugar, sucrose, dextrose, fructose, agave nectar, corn syrup, etc., in them. You are already sweet enough without these! ☺

Stick to the natural sugars found in most organic fruits and some organic vegetables to help fuel your body. Even use those in moderation to keep your blood sugar in balance.

Simply put, refined sugars are toxic. Start seeing them as poisons for your body, and wean yourself off of them as quickly as possible.

Refined sugars help cause heart disease and diabetes, feed cancer, and contribute to a host of many other physical and psychological issues. They are probably in 75% or more of the foods you are currently eating and drinking. Many food companies, in business to make a profit, understand the addictive properties of sugar, and add it to keep you coming back for more!

It is critically important to <u>always</u> read all the ingredients of the foods and drinks you are choosing, even when they are labeled "organic" or "all-natural." If you don't recognize an ingredient or can't pronounce it, your body won't know what it is either!

If there is any refined sugar listed of any kind, PLEASE put it back on the shelf.

Beware of "Sugar Free" and "Diet" foods and drinks, too, as they often have the 200-times-sweeter-than-sugar ingredients of aspartame in them to make you want them even more, with names like "AminoSweet," "Splenda," "NutraSweet," "Equal," etc. - all really nasty and potentially dangerous stuff.

(A side note about agave nectar - a "new" refined sugar used in many "health" foods today - and high fructose corn syrup. Both are made using a chemical process with genetically modified enzymes, caustic acids, clarifiers, filtration chemicals, etc. The result is a high level of refined fructose in the remaining syrup. "NuStevia" is a far safer alternative if you must have some added sweetness. Of course, eliminating all sweets/sugars from your diet is the best choice of all.)

In no particular order, here are **46** of the 146 reasons Nancy Appleton, Ph.D., gives to never eat refined sugars again:

- ✦ Sugar can suppress the immune system.

- ✦ Sugar can upset the body's natural mineral balance.

- ✦ Sugar can contribute to hyperactivity, anxiety, depression, concentration difficulties, and crankiness in children.

- ✦ Sugar can cause arthritis.

✦ Sugar can cause drowsiness and decreased activity in children.

✦ Sugar can reduce helpful high density cholesterol (HDLs).

✦ Sugar can promote an elevation of harmful cholesterol (LDLs).

✦ Sugar can cause hypoglycemia.

✦ Sugar contributes to a weakened defense against bacterial infection.

✦ Sugar can cause kidney damage.

✦ Sugar can increase the risk of coronary disease.

✦ Sugar can cause multiple sclerosis.

✦ Sugar can cause asthma.

✦ Sugar interferes with absorption of calcium and magnesium.

✦ Sugar can increase fasting levels of blood glucose.

✦ Sugar can promote tooth decay.

✦ Sugar can produce an acidic stomach.

✦ Sugar can raise adrenaline levels in children.

✦ Sugar can lead to periodontal disease.

✦ Sugar can speed the aging process, causing wrinkles and gray hair.

✦ Sugar can contribute to weight gain and obesity.

✦ Sugar can contribute to diabetes.

✦ Sugar can contribute to osteoporosis.

✦ Sugar can cause varicose veins.

✦ Sugar can cause hemorrhoids.

✦ Sugar can cause cardiovascular disease.

✦ Sugar can increase systolic blood pressure.

✦ Sugar can cause food allergies.

✦ Sugar can cause free radical formation in the bloodstream.

✦ Sugar can cause toxemia during pregnancy.

✦ Sugar can contribute to eczema in children.

✦ Sugar can overstress the pancreas, causing damage.

✦ Sugar can cause atherosclerosis.

✦ Sugar can cause appendicitis.

✦ Sugar can cause liver cells to divide, increasing the size of the liver.

✦ Sugar can increase kidney size and produce patho-
logical changes in the kidney.

✦ Sugar can cause depression.

✦ Sugar can increase the body's fluid retention.

✦ Sugar can cause hormonal imbalance.

✦ Sugar can cause hypertension.

✦ Sugar can cause headaches, including migraines.

✦ Sugar can cause an increase in delta, alpha, and
theta brain waves, which can alter the mind's ability to think clearly.

✦ Sugar can increase the risk of blood clots and
strokes.

✦ Sugar can cause gallstones.

✦ Sugar increases bacterial fermentation in the colon.

✦ Sugar can weaken eyesight.

I know, I know... a sugar addiction is difficult to overcome.
I was addicted once, too. Just remember, the intake of any
amount of sugar, even a tiny bit, usually leads to the craving
for more sugar. You really need to give up as close to 100%
as possible if you want optimal health over a lifetime.

The good news is that when the body gets the foods it <u>really</u> wants and needs, and it no longer has the refined sugar coming in, it will no longer crave it!

I have been amazed at how my body craves green veggies over sugar every day now. It takes a little time for the transition to happen, as every addiction has to go through a detox period, but it WILL happen. Stick with it. You CAN do this. YOU are worth it. Encourage all your family members to do the same.

To help your motivation, there is a fantastic movie called "Hungry For Change" that I highly recommend you watch. In a very entertaining and brilliant manner, it addresses the sugar issue and all sorts of other important pieces to the puzzle of good health.

Even the TV show "60 Minutes" shared this information about sugar and how toxic it is. You can find the segment hosted by Dr. Sanjay Gupta at www.cbsnews.com.

I believe with all my heart that the sooner we <u>all</u> get back to Nature in our eating and drinking of organic plant foods, pure water, and organic green juices, the sooner we will <u>all</u> be healthier and won't need so much health care reform!

Give refined sugars up for YOU, give them up for your family, give them up for your friends, and give them up for the world. We all want you here for a long time to come.

To your health and your already sweet enough self!

♥♥♥

WISDOM SNACK #14 - TOXINS

Unfortunately, we live in a toxic world.

The good news is there are plenty of things we can do to both protect and help heal our bodies, as well as protect and help heal our world. Many positive alternatives exist, so don't be discouraged.

Some things you should KNOW:

Your skin is the largest organ of the body, and it is more absorbent than you probably think. What you put on it matters. From Naturopath Jim Reese: "*Whatever you put on your skin will enter your blood stream within minutes. Once there, the substance is looked at by your body in two primary ways. First it will identify whether the substance is a nutrient that the cells and tissue need. Next it will determine if the substance is a toxin. If so, it tries to eliminate it."*

Samuel Epstein, MD, says, *"Chemicals taken in by the mouth are absorbed by the intestines and pass into venous blood, which is taken to the liver... carcinogens absorbed through the skin bypass the liver and enter blood circulation <u>without this protection</u>."*

Think about the creams. lotions, cosmetics, hair removal products, hair coloring, etc., that many of us use. A rule of thumb is to look at the ingredients on the side of the container, and if you wouldn't eat it, don't use it! Although it sounds funny, I'm not kidding.

Also think about swimming in pools, spas, or hot tubs that use chlorine, bromine, or other chemicals. Try your best not to do this. Instead, find natural, clean water sources, or pools and spas that use salt for their cleansing systems. Salt creates natural chloramines to kill bacteria when used correctly.

As mentioned in the previous "Water" Wisdom Snack, please do everything you can to get a whole house soft water system that uses salt to help filter out chemicals like chlorine and ammonia in tap water.

Find <u>truly</u> natural and organic cosmetics, nail care, and hair care products to use. Remember, read all of the ingredients! If you color your hair, there are organic color systems available now that are far healthier for both you and your hairdresser. Using natural enzymes, there are no toxic smells, they implode the hair shaft instead of exploding it, and take one-third the time to work than conventional hair coloring.

Always avoid anything with the words "fragrance" or "parfum" in the ingredients, as these words really mean synthetic chemicals. Avoid toxic ingredients in perfume, shampoo, fabric softeners, bleach, air fresheners, dishwashing liquid, laundry detergent, soap, hairspray, shaving cream, aftershave, deodorants, nail polish remover, and more.

The good news is there are plenty of natural, eco-friendly, healthier alternatives on the market today.

Remember, dear Wisdom Seeker, your goal is to continually be as close to Nature as possible. True long-term health and healing comes, as Kris Carr says, from what we eat, drink, and think - and we are "drinking" in everything we put on our skin or breathe through our noses.

Guess what?! The more I learned about organic, eco-friendly, healthy ways of living, the fewer products I brought into my home!

As my skin and health grew clearer and better from new ways of eating, drinking, and thinking, I found I needed fewer and fewer external products to look great, stay at the weight I wanted to be, and feel good. Wonderful!

This will happen for you as well, the longer you follow the suggestions in this 30-day program... and think of all the money you will save!

Some other toxic reminders:

+ Please avoid walking or running on heavily traveled streets where you are breathing in fumes from cars.

+ Find organic ways to work in your garden and never use toxic weed killers or poisons of any kind.

+ Wear quality respirators or masks that truly prevent inhalation of dust particles, paint, spray mists, fumes, and solvents when doing woodworking, artwork, crafts with glues, etc. Always try to use the least toxic, most organic products possible.

✦ When replacing your mattress, upholstery, or curtains, try to go organic. Truly organic mattresses, furniture, and fabrics are free of fire retardants, pesticides, dioxins, formaldehyde, and other chemicals that may damage health.

✦ Avoid certain fabrics and clothing such as acetate, acrylic, nylon, polyester, rayon, triacetate, and any materials promoted as permanent press, stain-proof, or static or wrinkle-resistant. Stick with wool, silk, hemp, or cotton. Today, even cotton can have issues, thanks to defoliants, pesticides, and insecticides. Therefore, go with 100% organic cotton as best you can.

✦ When purchasing a new car, keep in mind there are approximately 275 chemicals in car interiors that give off toxic fumes for six months to a year. To minimize ill effects, ventilate a new car by opening doors and windows for five minutes before entering, and keep the car out of the sun as much as possible.

✦ Limit plastic bottle use. If needed, only use BPA-free plastic bottles. (Bisphenol A is an industrial chemical used to make polycarbonate plastic resins, epoxy resins, and other toxic products.)

✦ Encourage your vendors to use BPA-free credit card receipt paper. This is a very easy switch, yet few businesses so far are doing it. Touching credit card receipt paper with BPA is toxic.

+ Avoid squishy plastics, as these contain toxic phthalates. Some products that should be avoided are: vinyl windows and doors, PVC packaging, (if marked with the #3 recycling symbol, indicating it contains PVC), PVC toys, (like squishy rubber duckies), vinyl plastic wrap and food storage containers, and vinyl shower curtains.

The subject of heavy metals, a HUGE source of daily toxins, will be discussed in a later Wisdom Snack.

The last hundred years have seen the creation of a plethora of man-made toxins that never before existed on our earth. These toxins are putting our livers into overwhelm, as they constantly try to remove the toxins from our blood.

When was the last time you thought about your liver? I want you to LOVE your liver! Your liver works so hard for you, day in and day out. It will work for you as long as it possibly can. The less toxins it has to process, the better it will be. Take care of it, so it can take care of you.

One more quick note about toxins. Although we usually think of toxins as things that are bad for our bodies, it is worth remembering that there are toxins of the mind and of the spirit as well.

What we see on TV, in movies, in magazines, in video games, on the Internet, etc., all goes into our bodies and reacts with our nervous systems, our brains, and our hearts. These things affect us, deeply, on many levels.

Choose wisely in all areas of your life. Yes, it may seem overwhelming at first. It certainly did for me! Yet as you keep making the shifts, one by one, you will feel better about your health, about the health of your family, and about the health of our planet.

To your clean, pure, natural, healthy self!

♥♥♥

WISDOM SNACK #15 - MONEY

"Money is neither my god nor my devil.
It is a form of energy
that tends to make us more of who we already are,
whether it's greedy or loving."
- Dan Millman

Did you grow up thinking that "money is the root of all evil?" Do you believe people with vast sums of money are greedy and therefore one needs to be poor or struggling to be socially conscious?

Time to let all of that thinking GO, and see money as the root of all GOOD instead.

Why? Because money is actually just energy, which is limitless, and it is LOVE in a tangible form. The more we have, the more GOOD we can do with it. Focus on how YOU use it, not on how others use it. The more we lead by example, the better. Remember, the more you give LOVE, the more it comes back to you... in all forms. Release those old money paradigms, and GROW with the flow!

We are energy beings. Everything around us is vibrating at an energetic level, too - from the sun to the oceans to a jet airplane to a tree to a rock. It is all energy. Those little colored pieces of currency or coin transferring between us to purchase goods and services are also energy - just energy.

Yes, the world will be a lovely place when we all go back to bartering our services and taking care of each other from birth to death in a kind and loving way. However, that paradigm does not exist... yet.

In our current paradigm, money is the means of exchange for most of our food, clothing, and shelter, so we need to see it for what it really is - a means to give to ourselves and to each other... as LOVE.

If you are operating from a level of "lack thinking" - believing you can never succeed in a down economy, or you are not worth over a certain amount of income, or you may become someone else if you make over six figures, or whatever other "less than" thoughts you have about your relationship with money - you will live in "lack."

If you are operating from a level of "abundant thinking" - believing there is always more than enough for your needs and for your ability to help others - watch money start to FLOW your way with grace and ease!

There is a wonderful author I highly recommend for helping you shift to abundant thinking - Chellie Campbell. Chellie will give you great, fun, and practical ways of doing so. Check out her brilliant books "The Wealthy Spirit - Daily Affirmations for Financial Stress Reduction," and "From Zero to Zillionaire." They are worth every penny. You may also get Chellie's "Free 30 Days to a Wealthy Spirit" by signing up on her home page at www.chellie.com.

Another great book for learning more about money's true source and meaning is Barbara Wilder's "Money is Love - Reconnecting to the Sacred Origins of Money."

Remember, you have permission to be healthy and abundant in ALL areas of your life, even financially. Get the books... read them... do what they say... and allow yourself to receive. Imagine all the GOOD you are going to do in the world with those additional funds!

Here is a great affirmation to repeat daily, even if you don't believe it... yet.

"The ocean is lavish with its abundance.
All my needs and desires are met before I even ask.
Good comes to me from everywhere and
everyone and everything."
- Louise Hay

To your financially abundant and healthy self!

NOTE: *"The greatest wealth is health."* (Virgil) KNOW that along with shelter and necessary clothing, the most important money you will ever spend throughout life is the money you spend on healthy organic food, pure water, and other ways to keep your mind, body, and spirit well - like yoga, massage, Bach Flowers™, Saladmaster cookware that does not leach toxins and metals into your food, and proper exercise. Same goes for your family, including pets. Don't skimp - you will pay far more for ill health in the long run if you do. Check your priorities. Budget, first and always, for your health.

WISDOM SNACK #16 - FOOD, WEIGHT, HEALTH

"The food you eat can either be
the safest and most powerful form of medicine,
or the slowest form of poison."
- Ann Wigmore

This Wisdom Snack could easily be a Wisdom Buffet, but I will try to keep it as succinct as possible and still give you the most important basics.

I don't KNOW of any other way to say this, so I will just say it...

If you are like most Americans, you are eating the Standard American Diet (S.A.D. - a most appropriate acronym)... and it is killing you. Oh, and probably just about everything you learned in school about nutrition and healthy eating was wrong.

We have been fed a steady "DIE-t" of misinformation all our lives. Now you will learn how to create a "LIVE-it" that is so simple, so natural, and so healing you may not believe it at first.

Many of the following "do's and don'ts" I learned from the Naturopath who saved my life, Jim Reese - a man who has saved and helped heal literally thousands of lives over the last thirty years.

All of the information below has been carefully and extensively researched by Jim and others for decades, and there are myriad reasons why the statements are written as they are.

Take baby steps if you need to, but start with as much as you can as soon as you can. The more you follow this "LIVE-it," the more you can see positive shifts happen in your health!

Here it is in an organic nutshell:

+ As best you can, stop eating and drinking man-made and processed foods. Remember, if Nature didn't make it, don't eat it.

✦ Stop eating and drinking foods that have been grown with pesticides and chemicals. Avoid all genetically modified foods as well. (GMOs)

✦ As best you can, stop eating foods that are cooked over 190 degrees. Over that temperature you lose most, if not all, of the enzymes and nutrients.

✦ Stop cooking in pots and pans that bring heavy metals into your food, which is nearly every pot and pan in America, no matter what the cost. Seriously. (More on that in a later Wisdom Snack.)

✦ As best you can, stop eating foods that are packaged.

✦ As best you can, stop eating and drinking anything that comes from an animal, fish, or bird.

✦ As best you can, stop eating and drinking anything acidic, which includes coffee, vinegars, tomatoes, citrus, beans, etc.

✦ As best you can, stop eating sugars of all kinds. (You already KNOW this, you clever Wisdom Seeker!)

✦ If you suffer from Arthritis or any pain and/or inflammation, eliminate the nightshade vegetables forever - tomatoes, eggplant, peppers, white potatoes, etc. (Red potatoes are better, if you must have a potato.) I had degenerative arthritis in L4, L5, and S1 in my spine for ten years that was often debilitating, and doctors told me it would only get worse and there was nothing that could be done. To my surprise, working with Jim and eliminating the nightshades cured it. No more pain since 2009 - amazing!

✦ Eat an organic plant-based diet for ALL your meals.

✦ Watch the entertaining and wonderful film "Fat, Sick, and Nearly Dead," even if you are none of those three things! Then start juicing organic green veggies daily. Go easy on the spinach, kale, and chard, though, as these have oxalates that are hard on certain organs of your body, especially the kidneys. (If you have kidney issues, or are prone to kidney stones, do not eat or drink these at all.) If you are not 100% healthy, (and who is these days), start juicing only with Romaine Lettuce, Cucumber, Celery, and Zucchini or any Yellow Squash. These will help heal and cleanse you.

✦ Eat vegetables and fruits in their pure, raw, organic form as often as possible. Exceptions are the cruciferous veggies like broccoli, cauliflower, cabbage, etc., as these are easier to digest when cooked a tiny bit. Eat fruits rarely, and never if you have cancer. Cancer feeds on any form of sugar, even fructose.

✦ Read labels on any packaged foods you do buy. The first ingredient listed is the highest content, the second ingredient listed is the second highest, and so on. Beware of salts and sugars in any processed foods.

✦ Know that beans and legumes are acidic, so only use them if they are organic <u>and</u> sprouted.

✦ Make your own salad dressings with pure water, fresh organic herbs, blended up veggies, a squeeze of lemon only for taste, and a little 100% Virgin Organic Olive Oil. You don't want more than three tablespoons of oil a day, so go easy on oils, space the three tablespoons out, and <u>never</u> heat them. The only recommended oils are 100% Virgin Organic Olive Oil, Organic Virgin Coconut Oil, and Organic Flax Oil - unless you have an allergy to flax.

✦ Sadly, arsenic has recently been found in all forms of rice, even organic. Best to stick only with Quinoa, Amaranth, and Millet for grains. Along with proteins, they should only be up to 25% on your plate, in four ounce amounts. The rest should be healthy, organic veggies!

(A note about allergies - the good news is that most, if not all, can clear up when your body is working the way it is meant to work.)

In addition to the film "Fat, Sick, and Nearly Dead," please also watch "Hungry For Change" and "Forks Over Knives." In my opinion, everyone on Planet Earth should watch these three films for knowledge about how to help heal and prevent illness. They are riveting, uplifting, entertaining, educational, and inspiring!

In today's toxic world, vitamins and supplements are also needed to sustain our organs and cells properly. As one example, with so many people working indoors, extra Vitamin D is usually recommended.

However, it is not wise to blindly choose vitamins and supplements without first getting tested by a Naturopath. Everyone is different, and choosing incorrect or inferior products may actually be detrimental rather than beneficial.

You may work long distance by phone with Jim Reese, (www.thereesewellnesssystem.com), or find a Naturopath where you live - but do find a good one to test you and work with you.

Remember, the most important money you will ever spend in your life is the money you spend on what you eat, drink, and do to help your health and peace of mind. Do not scrimp in these areas.

It is far less expensive to prevent illness and disease than to treat illness and disease. The foods and drinks you put in your mouth matter. Every single one. Choose wisely!

An extra BONUS from eating the "LIVE-it" way is one's weight tends to become what it should be, and it can maintain at that level! I lost 23 pounds when I made the switch, and have kept that weight off since early 2009, easily and effortlessly!

For those who struggle with extreme weight issues, such as obesity or anorexia/bulimia, KNOW that while making this shift will work wonders, you still need to work on what is eating YOU emotionally as well.

The one thing we can control is what we do or don't put into our mouths, so control or lack thereof tends to be a big behind-the-scenes issue for many of us.

Please work with someone qualified to help you discover the core issues you carry so you may release them naturally once and for all (ideally without drugs) and come back to life. I am available for holistic sessions by phone for such work, if you like.

Remember - eat light, think light, BE light.

Oh, and don't forget that what you do for you and your family extends to your pets, too!

Dogs and cats in the wild don't hunt for wheat, rice, chemicals, preservatives, and fillers. The more of these things that they consume in today's world, the more we see them dying from human diseases. They are meant to hunt and eat prey.

Explore raw diets for them. You can make your own, or use one of the many wonderful organic raw pet food companies throughout the United States. Many will ship the food in a frozen state right to your door. A good book for pet owners to read is "Natural Nutrition for Dogs and Cats" by Kymythy Schultze. I also suggest finding holistic veterinarians, of which thankfully there are more and more, who understand the raw food diet and healing from a more natural approach.

To you and your <u>entire</u> family's phenomenal health!

♥♥♥

WISDOM SNACK #17 - BACH FLOWERS™

"Health is our heritage, our right.
It is the complete and full union
between soul, mind, and body.
This is not a difficult, far-away ideal
to attain, but one so easy and natural
that many of us have overlooked it."
- Dr. Edward Bach, 1933

I believe with all my heart that if people knew about, understood, and used the all-natural Bach Flower™ essences when appropriate, there would be little to no need for anti-depressants in the world, along with many other medications.

Really.

It is a medical fact that emotional stress impacts health and well-being. When you can reduce your stress and deal with the emotions causing it - emotions like anger, jealousy, envy, bitterness, fear, worry, impatience, guilt, revenge, obsession, hopelessness, depression, hatred, regret, boredom, mood swings, panic, self-reproach, trauma, shock, grief, resentment, sadness, pessimism, irritation, disappointment, and blame - health invariably improves.

It is said that "DIS-ease" creates disease. So true. When we hold negative emotions, they "eat" away at us, often causing the body to manifest cancer, heart disease, and other illnesses.

Creating ease is always the goal, no matter what is going on in life. The Bach Flowers™ help us do that, every time we use them.

"Health depends on being in harmony with our souls."
- Dr. Edward Bach

In use for over 75 years in over 60 countries, Bach Flower™ essences help reverse nearly every negative state of human emotions. These simple, non-toxic, non-addictive, natural liquid preparations are entirely complimentary with all other medical and non-medical healing therapies, and they have no side effects. Each of the 38 essences Dr. Bach discovered work with a specific emotional state.

As a Bach Flower™ therapist making customized "Emotion Potions" for clients since 1998, I am consistently amazed by the magic of Nature in these essences... and the profound effects they have on shifting from the above negative list to positive emotions and actions of forgiveness, love, acceptance, gratitude, tolerance, joy, patience, support, peace, calm, happiness, creativity, enthusiasm, optimism, contentment, respect, hopefulness, empowerment, appreciation, freedom, and passion... to name just a few!

The Bach Flowers™ may be used with adults, children, newborn babies, pets, and even limp plants! If someone is in recovery, we suggest they spray the essences around them rather than taking the drops internally - they will still have the same effect.

Perhaps you have heard of "Rescue Remedy." This is a combination of five of the essences specific for stress, grief, trauma, sadness, etc. It is a good idea to have a bottle on hand at all times. There is also a version of it called "Rescue Sleep" to take before bed if you are having trouble sleeping, as well as "Rescue Energy," which is <u>far</u> better for you than those unhealthy energy drinks! These may all be found at most health food stores.

To learn more about the Bach Flowers™, please visit my website at www.kathychism.com. The more you KNOW, the happier and healthier you will GROW!

To your blooming, calm, healthy, harmonious self!

♥♥♥

WISDOM SNACK #18 -
YOUR STORY

We ALL have our stories. Our "what ifs," "if only's," and "why me?" tales of woe.

I have my story. You have your story. A great many of us stay stuck in our stories for a lifetime... yet here is the BIG SECRET:

YOU ARE NOT YOUR STORY, AND IT ALL HAD TO HAPPEN TO BRING YOU TO EXACTLY WHERE YOU ARE TODAY!

Now, get ready to let GO of regrets, anger, guilt, resentment, sorrow... and finally BE free.

A client asked me recently, "Yes, but how? It is so hard!" I told her you simply choose to always fly your F.L.A.G. of Forgiveness, Love, Acceptance, and Gratitude - for yourself, for all others, (no exceptions), and for what is.

No matter what.

> *"When you blame others,*
> *you give up on your power to change."*
> - Author Unknown

People often get stuck in "if only" mode.

+ "If only my spouse would behave a certain way, my life would be better."

+ "If only my parent hadn't done such and such, then I could have been someone."

+ "If only my employer would do this or that, my job would be bearable."

+ "If only the economy would improve, then I would have money."

+ "If only the news on TV was better, I wouldn't be so scared all the time."

Any of those sound familiar?!

"If only's" don't do anything except hold you back from being who YOU really are. YOU have ultimate control over your life by the choices YOU make NOW.

Choose to stop blaming and wishing things were different, and get your TRUE power back. We have a short time on this earth. Why waste it being upset?

What is, is.

What was, was.

Be grateful for the lessons, breathe them out, and let them GO.

Time to move on... and be the REAL you: joyful, healthy, loving, and abundant!

A friend asked me once how to really feel love.

I answered simply, "Open your heart."

He said his heart was closed due to a variety of past circumstances. I reminded him that was only his story, not the real him.

He agreed to:

+ let go of his story

+ be vulnerable

+ live in the now

+ truly understand that we are <u>all</u> connected as ONE - so in order to love another, one must love oneself first

It is all pretty simple, once you get the hang of it. The more you do these things, the easier life gets.

Come from LOVE, always and in all ways. This makes it so much easier for true love to find YOU.

"It's never too late to have a happy childhood."
- Berke Breathed

If you created a persona in grade school, high school, college, or beyond that became a "you" that you no longer like or want to be, KNOW you can recreate yourself at any time. You are not your previous actions, you are not your past mistakes, you are not whatever people may think of you, nor are you who they think you should be.

You are YOU, and the sooner you become your authentic self, the sooner your life can change for the better. When I finally became me, I lost some friends and family who didn't like or understand the change... yet my "heart family" has grown beyond my wildest dreams.

BE who YOU really are. Feel great in your own skin. Your true friends will love you all the more, and best of all, YOU will love you all the more as well.

No matter what happened or what you did on your path as a child, young adult, or adult, once you let it all GO and forgive mistakes made by yourself and others, you are finally FREE to BE the fun-loving, joyous, energized, amazing soul you were born to be.

Being happy is your birthright. Why waste any more time being otherwise?!

> *"To constantly think of the times*
> *when your life was not amazing*
> *really robs one of the joy of the good parts...*
> *and of NOW."*
> - Rosie O'Donnell

KNOW the past is simply that - the past. Again, it all had to happen to make you the fabulous, beautiful, kind, loving, wonderful soul that you are today.

Forgive it, Love it, Accept it, be Grateful for it (F.L.A.G.)... and move on. IT IS TIME to let the past GO, and create a new world for yourself and all around you.

To happy, healthy, positive, reborn YOU!

♥♥♥ *Kathy*

WISDOM SNACK #19 - HEAVY METALS

You have already learned about toxins in our environment. This Wisdom Snack is to give you some details about heavy metal toxins such as lead, mercury, and arsenic found in our air, water, soil, and so many of the products we use.

Do not despair! By the end of this Wisdom Snack you will have simple solutions for these heavy metals that can cause so many health issues - issues like high blood pressure, anemia, kidney damage, memory and learning difficulties, digestive problems, etc.

The good news is there are two ways you may easily counteract many of the heavy metals we all encounter just by being alive today on Planet Earth.

#1. The first is an incredible, natural, non-toxic zeolite product called "Natural Cellular Defense 2" (NCD2) by Waiora that removes the heavy metals and toxins from your body, supports your immune system, and helps balance pH levels in your body as well.

From the Waiora website:

"For centuries, the powdered forms of specific zeolites have been used as traditional remedies throughout Asia to promote overall health and well-being. The story of 'volcanic rocks' has been passed down from generation to generation as more and more people have experienced its life-changing benefits.

Zeolites are natural volcanic minerals with a unique, complex crystalline structure. Its honeycomb framework of cavities and channels (like cages) works at the cellular level, trapping heavy metals and toxins. In fact, because it is one of the few negatively charged minerals in nature, zeolites act as magnets drawing toxins to it, capturing them in its cage and removing them from the body."

Taking NCD2 is easy.

The first day, take three drops in an 8 oz. glass of water in the morning.

The second day, do the same in the morning, and again in the afternoon.

The third day, do the same in the morning, in the afternoon, and in the evening.

Stick with this three-times-a-day routine from then on.

#2. The second way to counteract heavy metals is to learn about your cookware. Pots and pans? Really? Yes.

According to the Cookware Manufacturer Association (CMA), there are no regulations on cookware in the United States. Many of the pots and pans sold in America are actually illegal in other parts of the world, due to the health issues!

Don't be fooled by higher costs somehow making certain pots and pans "better." Cost has nothing to do with the leaching of heavy metals into your foods. We have also been led to believe, incorrectly, that certain cookware, (like cast iron, for example), is somehow "good" for us... which couldn't be further from the truth.

You as a Wisdom Seeker following this 30-Day Program already understand how toxins are seeping into nearly everything we touch, breathe, smell, etc. Well, when almost all cookware is heated, toxins and/or metals leach into our air and/or our foods, too.

Here are some things you should KNOW, compiled from the Federal Aviation Agency Occupational Health & Safety Bulletin, the Brandywine Science Center, and the Cookware Manufacturer Association.

+ All **Non-Stick** cookware is toxic. When heated, toxic gasses and particles result that can create severe lung damage and death in birds. It can also create flu-like symptoms in humans, including sore throat, fever, chills, shortness of breath, tightness of chest, headaches, general malaise, and coughs.

+ **Cast Iron** is the most porous of all metals. It can contain bacteria and rancid, carcinogenic heated oils in the pores. Contrary to popular belief, the human body cannot assimilate the ferric iron from a cast iron pan. Ferric iron reacts with the peroxides in the body, producing harmful free-radicals.

+ **Enamel** cookware is fused glass, made with cadmium, boron, and lead... which can cause neurological damage.

+ Most **Stainless Steel** allows chrome and nickel to bleed into foods as the salts and acids of the food react with the pot. Only high-grade surgical stainless steel does not.

✦ **Aluminum** cookware, including anodized aluminum, is prohibited in Germany, France, Belgium, Great Britain, Switzerland, Hungary, and Brazil. All vegetables cooked in aluminum produce hydroxide poison, which neutralizes digestive juices, causing a deficiency in digestion. This can lead to stomach and gastrointestinal troubles.

✦ **Glass** and **Porcelain** cookware both use boron and lead in their manufacturing process. As the cookware is heated, leaching occurs.

I only recommend using "Saladmaster" cookware, which is composed of 316Ti surgical grade titanium stainless steel - just like what you would get with a knee replacement in your body. No leaching of anything. Period. Plus, the pans are designed to keep nutrients _in_ food with their unique cooking system that actually uses far lower temperatures... and due to their design and quality, they have the added bonus of cooking food twice as fast!

The design of the pots and pans is brilliant on many more levels as well. Beware of any you find on places like Craigslist, though, as often these are fakes that have come in from overseas. Saladmaster cookware is made in the U.S.A.

As Saladmaster pots and pans are considered health care products, they are not sold in any stores, online, or through a multi-level marketing system. Instead, they are sold through educators like me, many of whom work hand-in-hand with Dr. Neal Barnard, The Cancer Project, etc.

When educating about the Saladmaster products, I am often met with an exclamation of, "Wow - they are so expensive!" My reply is that cancer is far more expensive, and to think about the cost of even a small amount of surgical steel when it is used for surgeries. In reality, the pans are reasonable, and pay for themselves many times over as they continually produce healthy, high-quality food, and easily last for generations.

People will spend thousands upon thousands of dollars to create beautiful kitchens, yet often scrimp when it comes to the purchase of some of the most important items in those kitchens - their pots and pans. Often it is simply because they do not KNOW the health risks of these items.

Now YOU do.

To your pure, strong, clean-cooking, healthy self!

♥♥♥ *Kathy*

WISDOM SNACK #20 - MEDITATION

"Imagine a temple inside your mind,
a haven from the chaos of the world.
Visit often."
- Marianne Williamson

I told a great sage once that I was terrible at meditation... that my brain has a hard time shutting down, and I get distracted easily by the thoughts that pour in.

She asked, "Do you KNOW anyone who is GOOD at meditation? No! That's why they call it a practice! If someone was good at it, they would only have to do it once in their lifetime. Even Zen Buddhist monks do it daily."

Find a quiet space, close your eyes, focus on deep breathing, and when thoughts come in, let them float by like clouds. You have an "inner sanctuary." Go there for at least ten minutes a day, and it will get easier and easier to find a place of calm, peace, and inspiration.

Here are Ten Reasons to Meditate Daily from Kristin Shepherd:

1. You become clearer and calmer.
2. Your blood pressure lowers.
3. People around you enjoy your company.
4. Your connection with Source is strengthened.
5. You achieve several hours of sleep in one 20-minute session.
6. Problems suddenly have clear solutions.
7. Productivity skyrockets.
8. You enjoy increased life expectancy.
9. You experience stress reduction.
10. You feel fantastic all day!

A friend shared an adorable little video with me, and it is PERFECT for anyone who feels they can't learn to meditate. Search You Tube online for "One-Moment Meditation - How to Meditate in a Moment," and choose the fun line-drawing video that pops up. It will help you learn how to shift anger, fear, stress, or anything else you would like to release... in literally a moment, any-where, any time!

Even ten minutes a day visiting your "inner sanctuary" is a proven stress reducer. Bonus: answers will often come to you easily once you simply let the questions GO.

You may be thinking, "I just don't have the time to meditate." Amazingly, doing this daily practice actually creates <u>more</u> time in your life, as strange as that may sound. Make the time. You'll KNOW what I mean once you start doing it! ☺

To your calm, peaceful, meditative self!

♥♥♥ *Kathy*

NOTE: You just never KNOW from where or whom a great lesson will come. A few years ago, I had to call a computer software repair line, and was connected to a lovely gentleman in India. After he heard my issue, he politely said he needed to put me on hold, and ended that statement with four profound words: **"Please enjoy the silence."**

Loved it! Have YOU enjoyed any silence lately?! In our busy, "get-it-done," noisy world, enjoying some silence daily can really ground you, center you, and open you to new ideas and ways to become more happy, healthy, prosperous, etc.

Please, enjoy some silence. Now. Daily. Breathe... ahhhhhhhhhhhhh.

WISDOM SNACK #21 - GREEN JUICING

Have you seen the movie, "Fat, Sick, and Nearly Dead" yet?

Strange title name... and yet KNOW it is one of the best movies for health ever! It is a really fun and engaging film, and even if you are none of those three words, I <u>highly</u> recommend it for knowledge and inspiration around the wonders of juicing, weight loss, and life.

One of the three "stars" of the movie is actually a Breville juicer!

I believe the three most important "must-have" kitchen appliances are a refrigerator, a blender, and a juicer. Along with your stove and Saladmaster pots and pans, these three items can assist your health better than any other appliance in your kitchen, so invest in them now. Purchase quality that will last over time, as you will use them a LOT.

So, what is the big deal about organic green juicing?

Well... think about this. Wild chimpanzees have an extremely strong natural immunity to AIDS, Hepatitis C, Cancer, and other fatal human diseases. They share an estimated 99.4% of genes with humans, yet they consume <u>significantly</u> more green leaves that most humans.

In today's world, we usually do not have time to consume vast plates and bowls filled with greens all day long to get the vitamins, nutrients, and phytonutrients we need. We are also being bombarded by toxins from all areas of life that need to get processed through the body and removed. Hard work for the liver and other organs. Soooooooo...

+ Organic green juices contain high levels of chlorophyll, which is a powerful phytonutrient that attaches to toxins and heavy metals and helps remove them from your body.

✦ Organic green juices allow us to take in great quantities of veggies at once, easily absorbing their nutrients.

✦ Organic green juices go straight into your bloodstream, which carries all the nutrients to where they are needed the most in your body without possible delays in digestion. (Many people have digestion issues due to poor food choices and stress throughout life. Green juices can help cure these issues, and therefore assist the body in proper functioning.)

✦ Organic green juices stimulate red blood cell production, which assists the blood's ability to carry oxygen.

✦ Organic green juices are incredible for cleansing the body of toxins and waste.

✦ Organic green juices can bring more variety of vegetables into your diet, as you may not want to eat something alone, but won't mind it mixed into a juice.

✦ Organic green juicing takes very little time to do each day... perfect for our busy lives.

✦ Organic green juices are fun for the whole family to create. Call them "Superman" or "Wonder

Woman" juices for your children and watch them respond!

✦ Organic green juices taste great, and you feel GOOD just knowing you are doing something so wonderful for your body and for your family!

As you are a Wisdom Seeker striving to learn all about your body so that you may take better care of it, below is some fantastic info about phytonutrients... and organic green juicing is an easy way to get these vitally important keys for health.

From the Glyconutrients reference site:

> *"Phytonutrients are nutrients derived from plant material that have been shown to be necessary for sustaining human life. Their role in plants is to protect plants from disease, injuries, insects, drought, excessive heat, ultraviolet rays, and poisons or pollutants in the air or soil. They form part of the plant's immune system.*
>
> *Phytochemicals are associated with the prevention and/or treatment of at least four of the leading causes of death in Western countries - Cancer, Diabetes, Cardiovascular Disease, and Hypertension. They are involved in many processes, including ones that*

help prevent cell damage, prevent cancer cell repli-
cation, and decrease cholesterol levels.

One of the most important groups of phytochemi-
cals are the phytosterols, or phytohormones as
they are sometimes known. They act to modulate
the human endocrine system.

One of the most important human sterols is
Dehydroepiandrosterone (DHEA). This hormone
is produced in our adrenal glands and serves a
variety of functions. It is often called the 'mother'
hormone, as it has the ability to convert itself into
other hormones such as estrogen, testosterone,
progesterone, and corticosterone, on demand.

Scientific research reveals that adequate DHEA in
the body can slow the aging process, and prevent,
improve, and often even reverse conditions such
as Cancer, Heart Disease, Memory Loss, Obesity,
and Osteoporosis. DHEA blood levels peak between ages 20 to 25 years and then decline with
age in both men and women.

DHEA is the precursor of stress hormones such as
cortisol and adrenaline. When our body makes these
hormones, DHEA levels decline. With our stressful
lives it is no wonder that most people have deficient

levels of DHEA... hence creating the medical conditions and degenerative diseases listed above."

Here is the thing. The body will always try to maintain health for as long as it can. It wants to serve you and take care of you. However, it can only do so much without your help. At some point, it will not be able to handle the toxic overload, and disease will enter.

Please, do everything you can to let it help you. Daily organic green juices are some of the best things you can ever do for it... and therefore, for YOU.

There are four ingredients you may always put in your juices that will be both very nutritive and helpful for cleansing toxins:

+ Organic Celery

+ Organic Cucumber

+ Organic Zucchini (green or yellow)

+ Organic Romaine Lettuce

In addition, dandelion greens are wonderful for cleansing the liver, and they help the body in many other ways, too. As dandelion greens can be a bit bitter, you may add purple or golden beets to sweeten things up once in a while. (Careful, though, as too many beets add to our sugar levels.) I also add a tiny bit of ginger, carrots, and/or parsnips from time to time as well.

Go easy on the spinach, kale, and chard, please, and only have one of those once a week, if at all. About 80% of kidney stones formed by adults in the U.S. are composed of calcium oxalate, found in these veggies.

When you begin juicing, you may go through what is called a "toxic cleanse" as your body starts to slough off unwanted toxins... which is a good thing!

Depending on how toxic your body is, this may manifest as mild to severe headaches, or fever, or nausea, or diarrhea, etc., lasting anywhere from one day to two weeks. Many have no reactions at all. When I started juicing, I had three days of mild headaches. Keep some Essentia Water on hand for any of these situations in case they occur, and try not to take aspirin or any drugs for them so the body is not confused by what to cleanse.

Although you are simply putting healthy organic veggies into your body, current norms compel me to mention that if you are currently under a doctor's care or taking prescription drugs or insulin, please advise your doctor of what you want to do before starting.

Having said that, sadly, most U.S. doctors are not given training in medical school about nutrition more than a two or three hour class in four to seven years of training... and that class is usually not about plant-based diets, so they may not truly understand the importance of organic green juicing.

My own experience, and that of all my clients, friends, and family who have started organic green juicing regularly, is the possible short toxic cleanse is <u>well</u> worth any mild or brief discomfort in order to have improved and glowing health on the other side - ideally for a lifetime!

To your clean, green, juicy self!

♥♥♥ *Kathy*

NOTE: Wheatgrass is also fantastic for humans, yet needs to be juiced in a different manner. With wheatgrass, if you don't have a specific juicer for it, use a blender. From the Livestrong Foundation:

✦ Cut the wheatgrass stalks with a sharp pair of scissors just above the soil, or just above the root system of hydroponic wheatgrass.

✦ Place the wheatgrass stalks in the canister of the blender and add an equal amount of water. You may also use more water for a milder, more palatable beverage.

✦ Blend on high for at least 60 seconds or until the wheatgrass is completely pulverized.

✦ Strain out the wheatgrass pulp by pouring the wheatgrass and water mix through a few sheets of cheesecloth. Discard or compost the pulp.

I find it very telling that two of the organic greens that are the very best for us, dandelion greens and wheatgrass, are so prevalent on our planet! Nature's gifts to us all...

WISDOM SNACK #22 - POSITIVE AFFIRMATIONS

*"If you realized how powerful your thoughts are,
you would never think a negative thought."*
- Peace Pilgrim

OK, this Wisdom Snack may sound a little woo-woo... but stay with me!

A lot of people discard the idea of positive affirmations. These are simply people who don't KNOW how to use them correctly... for if they did, they would be using them all the time!

Today, YOU will learn some simple techniques for affirming, visualizing, and manifesting dreams for your highest good.

I first learned about affirmations in the late 1970's from Shakti Gawain's wonderful book, "Creative Visualization." It is still the go-to book for such things, and I highly recommend it. So does Oprah Winfrey, who has seen the power of using Shakti's techniques in her own life.

My own experience is that affirmations can only work if they are put in present tense, with no negative words.

For example, if you are going to affirm better health, choose a statement like: "I AM 100% HEALTHY NOW" instead of "I will be healthy soon." That statement always puts it in the future, so it will stay in the future.

Don't use "I no longer have pain," either. The body hears the word "pain" and does not understand the word "no," so it keeps creating pain.

Notice I started the positive affirmation sentence with the words "I AM."

These are two of the most powerful words on the planet, and many believe they bring divine energy right through you. When you want to powerfully manifest something for yourself, using these words will greatly help the process!

Affirmations may be spoken aloud, or in your head, or written on notes to put all over your house, your car, your workspace, etc., to remind you to say them over and over. You are, in a sense, retraining your thought processes by doing this.

What most people don't realize is that they are affirming all the time, simply by speaking. It is important to catch yourself whenever you hear your voice saying things like, "I am so stupid," or "Nothing ever goes right for me," or "She hates me," or "We have no money," or "There is no hope for our world," and on and on and on.

Statements like these keep creating those paradigms in your life. Why do that?!

Shift your language to positive affirmations. For example, instead of "I am so stupid," shift to "I am brilliant and accurate and always make excellent decisions for my highest good."

Instead of "Nothing ever goes right for me," try "I am amazed at how I operate in the flow of life, and things go right for me 24/7!"

Instead of "She hates me," switch to something like "I am loved by all who meet me, and I love everyone as well."

Instead of "We have no money," use "We are abundant and prosperous NOW. We comfortably have all our needs met and enjoy all the riches life has to offer."

Instead of "There is no hope for our world," state "The earth is a healthy planet, and is peopled by those who operate only from love and light."

Now you get the idea. Simple, clear, positive, present-tense statements. Even if you don't believe them, say them anyway.

See in your mind's eye what you want to have happen. Feel it happening. You may affirm on the go, or do a deep meditation first to really open up the space for what you want to manifest.

No matter how you do it, keep doing it. Don't give up just because what you want may not appear immediately. Everything happens in its right time.

I have witnessed many "miracles" in my own life and in the lives of many friends and clients from using positive affirmations.

You have nothing to lose by using them, and all of us have something to gain by your doing so!

To your positive, creatively-affirming, far happier self!

♥♥♥

WISDOM SNACK #23 - EMFs

EMFs are Electric and Magnetic Fields...
and they are nearly everywhere on earth.

"Artificial EMFs overwhelm your
body's own electrical fields,
changing frequency and distorting balance
of the body's electromagnetic field
and its communication systems.
This can cause physical, mental, and emotional chaos."
- Dr. Robert Becker

This Wisdom Snack is not meant to scare you, but rather to let you KNOW how pervasive these fields are so you may make educated decisions about how much you want to interact with them... as they all directly affect our health. Remember, knowledge is the best power you can ever use!

CELL PHONES

If you are someone who puts his or her cell phone up to your ear, please do NOT do that any more. Please, teach your children about this, too, as their growing brains are even more highly affected. Please do not wear your cell phone on your body, either. (Be careful about placing iPads, laptops, etc., on your body as well.)

Cell phone manufacturers even say in their directions to not put their phone up to your ear due to radiation! Keep your phone as far away from you as possible, using the speakerphone feature. If you must use a headset or earpiece, use one that is wired - NEVER a wireless Bluetooth.

Anderson Cooper and Dr. Sanjay Gupta spoke about this issue in earnest on CNN in a very important video. The TV show "60 Minutes" has also done a piece about the dangers of cell phone use. Please go to www.youtube.com and search for these - you will be amazed at how much proof is out there, yet it seems few people are paying attention. Please be one who does.

We are literally the canaries in the coal mine.

CELL PHONE TOWERS

Cell phone towers are also an issue. Want to find out how many cell phone towers and antennas are near you? Check out www.antennasearch.com. Time to move? Try to choose a place with only two or three of these towers and antennas max in a four mile radius of your home. If you can't move, spend time often in more EMF-free places... such as state parks, near the ocean, the desert, etc.

"There is strong evidence that EMFs and radio-microwave frequencies are associated with accelerated aging (enhanced cell death and cancer) and moods, depression, suicide, anger, rage, and violence - primarily through alteration of cellular calcium ions and the melatonin/seratonin balance."

- Dr. Neil Cherry of Lincoln University, New Zealand

I was getting severe headaches every time I worked on my computer, and they were becoming unbearable. Friend Marina James, a Certified Personal Trainer and Nutrition Consultant, suggested I get a "Harmonic Protector" to wear as a necklace, as she was doing. On her advice, although it sounded pretty woo-woo even for me, (and I can be a pretty woo-woo girl!), I bought one. That was in late 2010.

When I put it on as a necklace as suggested, it overpowered me, and my heart started going crazy... my body was just way too sensitive for it. On a whim, I decided to hang it next to my computer instead. Shazam! The headaches stopped, and I haven't had one since... and I work on my computer a LOT.

Go to www.worldwithoutparasites.com and search for "Harmonic Protector" if you would like to try one. It is far prettier in person, and the dolphin logo is lovely. I now have one for my car as well, and one hanging over my bed to help with sleep. This is particularly important if you use Wi-Fi at work or home. (Wi-Fi is another thing I highly recommend you DON'T use.)

Another wonderful company is Earthcalm at www. earthcalm.com. Check out their Quantum Cells for cell phones, and Nova Resonator necklaces in particular, to help combat EMFs.

DIRTY ELECTRICITY

Please also invest in a Stetzerizer Microsurge Meter at www.stetzerelectric.com to test all the electrical outlets at your home and work. Wherever you have an outlet with a reading of more than 50, place a Greenwave Dirty Electricity Filter there from www.greenwavefilters.com.

By the way, according to Jim Reese, tinnitus, (ringing in the ears), is becoming more and more prevalent, thanks to EMFs. If you are experiencing tinnitus, do everything you can to work with or eliminate the EMFs in your life.

The key is managing all these EMFs as best we can with the choices we make.

MICROWAVES

Are you still microwaving your food? Here are some things to KNOW, thanks to holistic health advocate Isis Melinda Israel Brock, who shares that Russian investigators found carcinogens were formed from the microwaving of nearly all tested foods:

+ The microwaving of milk and grains converted some of the amino acids into carcinogenic substances.

+ Microwaving prepared meats caused the formation of the cancer-causing agents d-Nitrosodienthanolamines.

+ Thawing frozen fruits by microwave converted their glucoside and galactoside fractions into carcinogenic substances.

+ Extremely short exposure of raw, cooked, or frozen vegetables converted their plant alkaloids into carcinogens.

+ Carcinogenic free radicals were formed in microwaved plants - especially root vegetables.

+ Ingestion of microwaved food causes a higher percentage of cancerous cells within the blood serum.

+ In a statistically high percentage of persons, microwaved food caused stomach and intestinal cancerous growths.

On top of all that, if you eat something within two minutes of it being microwaved, it is actually still cooking and can cook your esophagus as the food travels through it - yikes! Also, if you must microwave something, KNOW to never microwave anything in plastic or with a plastic covering, as the toxic chemicals from the plastic then enter your food.

Staying as close to Nature as possible with how and what we eat and drink is always better...

"SMART" METERS

One last EMF piece. Where I lived in California, we were almost forced to have "Smart Meters" put on our homes by the public utility company, even though health risks were proven. Thousands were put on homes without owners knowing.

Thanks to a huge outcry from the public, residents of California may now have them removed if they were put on, or may opt out of the program and keep their old meters. (Unfortunately, the utility company forces customers to pay extra no matter which choice is made.)

These "Smart Meters" are being installed now by utility companies across America, with lots of TV advertising about how "wonderful" they are. Please refuse to have one. Any meters within two miles of one's home will still affect you, so it is wise to get all your neighbors on board with their removal and prevention, too.

I happened to be home when a nice young employee of the utility company came to sneak one of these meters onto my house. I stopped him, and said I didn't want it. He started telling me all the reasons why I should want one.

When I explained the health risks to him, he got very quiet... and then said, "Maybe that's why ever since I started installing these I have had severe headaches, have felt dizzy, and am often nauseous."

I kindly suggested he find another job.

Newer is not necessarily better. The more we KNOW, the more we can make informed decisions about our health and the health of our families and friends.

To your naturally empowered healthy self!

♥♥♥

WISDOM SNACK #24 - LOSS, TEARS, GRIEF

This Wisdom Snack is actually a few Wisdom Snacklets wrapped up in one, as each Snacklet is equally important...

RELATIONSHIPS

There are times when it makes more sense to release a relationship rather than continuing to hang on to something that just isn't working, no matter how hard you tried, gave, worked, shared, and loved. You usually KNOW when it is time. If you have tried everything you can to make it work, yet it is making you physically, emotionally, and/or spiritually sick for an extended period, that is a pretty clear indication you might need to move on. Thank them for the lessons they taught you, always love them, and GO. Once you do that, the way is then open for someone or something created for your higher good to come in... and you are off to new adventures!

> *"How people treat you is their karma;*
> *how you react is yours."*
> - Wayne Dyer

No matter how difficult it may be at times to not get defensive when someone maligns you unjustly, take the higher ground. YOU know who you are, YOU know you are loving and kind, YOU know you always operate for the highest good of all. Keep coming from LOVE, speak in a kind manner, and/or, if necessary, bless them and send them on their way. KNOW there will always be plenty of others who understand and appreciate you. ♥♥♥

LOSS

Loss is inevitable. We are not fully alive without it. Therefore, it makes sense to embrace it rather than fight it, and find ways to fly our F.L.A.G.s about it. For example... several of my friends and clients recently lost their jobs - unexpectedly. The same thing happened once in my past, and I was crushed, confused, angry, and hurt at the time... only to later realize that if I had not been let go, something far better and more "me" would not have been able to show up in my life. I also found some jobs that I took along my path - ones that didn't seem to make much sense at the time - became invaluable experiences and provided necessary knowledge to work from later in life. KNOW that what looks like devastation and/or a waste of time is actually happening for your growth and opportunity. Like a phoenix, you, too, will rise from the ashes. ♥♥♥

REGRETS

Every single thing you have ever done in your life HAD TO HAPPEN to make you who you are today... so no regrets, OK? Also, KNOW that the choices you make today are creating who you will become tomorrow, so choose wisely. I AM choosing love, health, peace, and kindness... how about YOU? ♥♥♥

REJECTION

In my 20's I dreamed of being a flight attendant so I could see the world. For two straight years I applied to any airline that was hiring, with rejection after rejection after rejection. Finally, United Airlines had openings, and I was accepted. In the ten years I flew with them, every other airline I had applied with went out of business! Lesson to KNOW: What looks like rejection is often protection. ♥♥♥

HURT

"What other people think of me is none of my business."
- Unknown

I used to feel terribly hurt by remarks, lack of caring, and disappointments from expectations I held about friends, family, co-workers, etc. One day I finally woke up to the fact that not everybody was going to like me or what I am doing or have done with my life, no matter how hard I tried to make that happen... and that my job is to simply be who I am, do the best I can in the world, always come from LOVE, and let the rest GO. Whew - what a relief! I got lighter, brighter, more peaceful, and happier instantly with that one! KNOW you can, too. ♥♥♥

GRIEF

One of my clients was living in the past. She was mourning her parents, who had been dead for several years. She told me that if she moved on with joy instead of sadness, she was "leaving" them behind... a thought she could not bear. I told her to KNOW that by living with joy she is not leaving them, but rather LOVING and HONORING them always for giving her the gift of life. If you are carrying grief, change "leave" to LOVE and BE who the departed truly want you to be. It is time, and that time is NOW. ♥♥♥

TRAGEDY

When a tragedy hits close to home, it is easy to question humanity and succumb to depression and darkness. However, it is said that one lightworker can offset 70,000 of those in the dark. KNOW that it is critical to stay positive and in the light, no mater how scared or saddened you may feel... we all need you, Lightworker! ♥♥♥

BENEFITS OF TEARS

"There is a sacredness in tears.
They are not the mark of weakness, but of power.
They speak more eloquently than ten thousand tongues.
They are messengers of overwhelming grief...
and unspeakable love."
- Washington Irving

The human body is so amazing. Tear expert Dr. William Frey states that "Tears lubricate your eyes, remove irritants, reduce stress hormones, and contain antibodies that fight pathogenic microbes. Our bodies produce three kinds of tears: reflex, continuous, and emotional. Each kind has different healing roles."

KNOW it is not only OK to cry, it is actually GOOD for us - men and women alike, by the way. So when the tears come, let them FLOW... and take some Bach Flower™ "Star of Bethlehem" for grief, trauma, and sadness. ♥♥♥

I hope the Wisdom Snacklets above help you though difficult times...

To your powerful, healed, phoenix self!

♥♥♥ Kathy

WISDOM SNACK #25 - YOGA

In this Wisdom Snack, I want to share an amazing, inspirational, and personal story with you...

My parents divorced when I was young, and I lived alone with my mother from age seven until I left for college nine years later.

During that time, Mom rarely let me watch TV. Therefore, while home visiting during my senior year at college, I was surprised when she added a "TV Guide" to our cart at the grocery store.

I looked at her quizzically, and she simply said, "I don't know, I am just drawn to buying this today. I never have before."

The next day, she picked up the guide and it fell open to a show called "Yoga For Health" with Richard Hittleman. Mom watched the show, got down on the floor, and tried doing a few of the stretches.

I say "tried," because at age 60, this was a woman who was so arthritic she could barely bend over and touch her knees.

Mom had a hard life on many levels - from growing up in extreme poverty, moving 32 times with her family all before she finished high school, (including moves to a number of different states), experiencing a difficult marriage and divorce, etc.

By the time of this TV Guide moment, and for many years prior to this point, not only was she severely arthritic, she:

+ had a blood platelet count so low she was getting blood clots under her skin all over her body... and the doctors said if one happened near her heart, it would kill her

+ had bleeding ulcers, and doctors said she could not eat most fruits, nuts, and vegetables again - instead putting her on a diet mostly of things like baby food and cottage cheese

✦ was addicted to 18 different pain medications and anti-depressants - all prescribed by doctors

✦ had a heart murmur and an irregular heartbeat

✦ often suffered from severe migraine headaches that were immobilizing

✦ was manic depressive, and at one point had been institutionalized for six weeks and given shock treatments to her brain

Through these years she owned a delightful antique, music box, and gift shop, and was also an antique appraiser and very skilled artist. How she managed to function all those years I really don't know. A sense of responsibility and love as a mother is my best guess.

So there she was... this tired, sick, and often broken sweet woman, down on her living room floor trying to do some Hatha Yoga stretches to a TV program for whatever reason.

The next day she did it again.

The next day she did it again.

When the weekend rolled around and the show wasn't on, she did it again anyway... and again, and again, and...

In only one year of doing daily yoga:

+ Mom was off ALL her medications!

+ Her ulcers were gone!

+ Her arthritis was gone! She was doing headstands and was able to put her leg behind her head!

+ Her platelet count was normal! (All her doctors had said this would be impossible.)

+ She began eating all the foods doctors had said she would never eat again, like most vegetables, fruits, and nuts!

+ The headaches became very rare occurrences!

Her heart also improved, although ultimately she was fitted for a pacemaker some years later. (Sadly, we didn't know then what we know now about meat and dairy and the effects on the heart from those... although vegetarian, she still ate lots of dairy products.)

BEST of all, though, was the JOY she finally found at age 60 and beyond in living each day. The years and years of depression and suicide threats came to a halt.

Mom did yoga daily until age 75. She passed away in 1998 at age 81 of heart failure, in her sleep, the way she had always said she wanted to go when it was her time.

Talk about transformation.

Talk about a butterfly finally emerging from her cocoon.

What a lesson for me to witness first-hand... and KNOW forever more that ANY of us can change our lives at any time. WOW. I am eternally grateful to my mother for so, so much, including listening to her own heartpull to pick up a TV Guide that day and get down on the floor!

This story is to let YOU know that you can change for the better, too, no matter what is going on, and no matter what your age.

Do some yoga. Even just ten minutes of yoga stretching will lower your stress hormones of cortisol and adrenaline. It's worth doing just for that alone!

Take a class, watch a TV show or yoga DVD, whatever. Just do it.

Start every day with the yoga "Sun Salutation." Even if you can't perform it perfectly yet, do what you can. Each day, you <u>will</u> improve... just like Mom did.

To your limber, flexible, aligned, transforming, butterfly self!

♥♥♥

WISDOM SNACK #26 -
YOUR WORD

Think the little things you do or say don't matter?

Consider the "Butterfly Effect" - the idea that a butterfly's wings create tiny changes in the atmosphere that may ultimately alter the path of a tornado, or delay, accelerate, or even prevent the occurrence of a tornado in another location.

KNOW that everything you do matters. <u>Everything</u>.

BE YOUR WORD.

Think about how important that statement is. Many of us get frustrated because people often say one thing and do another. This can be a politician promising something to get elected and then doing the opposite when in office, to someone late for an appointment who keeps you waiting, to someone saying they will call you and they never do, to someone who borrows money and never pays you back, and on and on.

Now, imagine if everyone was true to their word, what a world we would live in! It starts with US.

Communicating and speaking your truth in a kind and loving manner is such a HUGE key to a happy, healthy life.

For example, when you make an appointment at a certain time, do everything in your power to keep that appointment. If for some reason you absolutely have to be late, contact the person waiting and apologize - always respect their time.

Remember, YOU are your word. If you consistently say or promise one thing and do another, people begin to distrust you, and they may be hurt by what is perceived as lack of caring. They distance from you, then you feel hurt, and the cycle spirals down.

When you always speak your truth from love and kindness, you never have to backtrack, you don't have regret about whatever you said, you don't have to remember what lie you told to whom, you don't compromise your own needs, etc. It's all GOOD.

Now, all the words you <u>use</u> matter, too.

On Facebook, for example, I see many posts coming from love and kindness, and many posts unleashing anger and hatred on others. KNOW that every written and spoken word has power and affects us ALL, just like the flap of a butterfly's wing. If you choose to write or speak words of hate, anger, vitriol, belittlement, etc., the words also hurt YOU. Deeply.

We are all ONE, so whenever we make fun of, tease, degrade, negate, come from anger, and/or make disparaging remarks about another human being, we are tearing ourselves down while also lowering the vibration of the entire planet. Just because others do it - even comedians - doesn't make it justifiable.

Truly coming from love and peace in all our thoughts and actions is the only answer. As Gandhi stated, let's BE the change we wish to see in the world, and make an agreement to consciously choose not to say anything bad about anyone ever again. Imagine the shifts that will take place as more and more follow our lead!

"Choose being kind over being right,
and you'll be right every time."
- Richard Carlson

Yes, we all see and hear things that we strongly disagree with and/or tear at our hearts. Yet the healthy choice is to ALWAYS come from LOVE and find <u>solutions</u> for these instead of advancing any downward spirals with words.

KNOW, however, that although we try to be all things to all people, are being our word, and coming from a place of love and kindness, we may be misunderstood from time to time.

Some people will think the worst of us when we are actually giving the best of us. Remembering the phrase "what other people think of me is none of my business," and sending them love from your heart will help get you through those difficult moments.

Again, ALWAYS come from LOVE, to everyone, while staying true to yourself and your needs... no matter what. Eventually they will understand. Or they won't. What is, is, and all you can do is be the best YOU that you can be.

Remember, <u>everything</u> boils down to love or fear. Write, speak, and be LOVE. It is the only path to peace, both within and without.

"Ho'oponopono" is an ancient Hawaiian practice of reconciliation and forgiveness. The book "Zero Limits" by Ihaleakala Hew Len and Joe Vitale about this practice brings to light eleven incredibly beautiful words of truth. I recommend using them often to soften upsets and open hearts:

I Am Sorry.
Please Forgive Me.
I Love You.
Thank You.

Simple, beautiful, powerful.

To your truthful, kind, and always-coming-from-love self!

♥♥♥ *Kathy*

WISDOM SNACK #27 - ERASING FEAR, ANGER, AND PAIN

"Fear is a darkroom where negatives develop."
- Usman B. Asif

Face your fears. KNOW they won't go away until you do.

Usually you discover that what you feared isn't as bad as all the worry that went into it.

Years ago, I started taking flying lessons. I dreaded the first time I had to practice stalling the engine, putting the nose down into a dive, then restarting the engine and pulling out of the descent... alone. I also dreaded taking the written portion of the test. However, I wanted to fly so badly, I did both, got my license to fly Cessna 172s and Piper 28s, and was EMPOWERED.

Face your fears. Don't let them steal your dreams.

> *"Life's problems wouldn't be called 'hurdles'*
> *if there wasn't a way to get over them."*
> - Author Unknown

KNOW there is always a way. Usually it is as simple as asking for help, something that doesn't come easily to many. It doesn't come easily to me, and yet, when I do, I am always deeply touched by the outpouring of love and ideas that are freely given. Try it. Just as you love to give, others love to give to you. Let those hurdles become mere stepping stones, and find an easier path.

> *"Worrying does not take away tomorrow's troubles...*
> *It takes away today's peace."*
> - Author Unknown

I was born to a worry queen, and I became a worry princess at an early age... growing into my full worry crown rather quickly. I can easily worry about anything in a heartbeat, and this ability has never been my friend. In recent years, I have come to KNOW the adage above, and learned to say things like "delete that thought" as worry shows up. I'm WAY more joyful now because of it! Use the delete button, and you will be, too. ☺

"Not the fastest horse can catch a word spoken in anger."
- Chinese Proverb

Staying angry or upset about your past and the people in it is like dragging twenty elephants behind you everywhere you go. Why would you want to do that? KNOW when you stay focused on the past or the future, you have no chance of truly enjoying today... and today really is all there is. You are here. Not there. BE where you are.

When someone is coming from anger, it is really insecurity and/or fear being expressed. Learn to step away from it instead of getting plugged in and having it escalate. See the little child within that person, who in some way wasn't acknowledged or supported, or hugged or loved, or was abandoned or was abused, or was hurt by whatever happened.

Keep coming from love, no matter how difficult that may be. If you can, get that person to begin taking 2-4 drops or sprays of Bach Flower™ "Holly," (found at health food stores), four times a day, particularly first thing in the morning and last thing at night. It will work wonders naturally to help clear his or her anger issues.

"Pain is inevitable. Suffering is optional."
- M. Kathleen Casey

Once after I spoke at an event, the next speaker, whom I had just met, dissed my chosen profession to the group. In the past, my reaction would have been one of anger, hurt, and defensiveness. Although shocked, I chose instead to come from love and forgiveness, because I now understand that when people do things like that, they are simply feeling inadequate and "less than." How lovely to just be able to let it GO, and to wish that person peace and healing.

You, too, can change "diss" to "bliss!"

Once you also KNOW in your heart that everything happens for a reason and happens exactly as it should, you no longer feel anger for what is. Instead, you get actively involved in finding loving and kind solutions to problems that arise.

This is one path to enlightenment... which is a lifelong journey. The sooner you can get on this particular path, the sooner things become easier in all areas of your life.

"Peace.
It does not mean to be in a place
where there is no noise, trouble, or hard work.

*It means to be in the midst of those things
and still be calm in your heart."*
- Author Unknown

To your brave, strong, sure, open, healthy, loving self!

♥♥♥

NOTE: A quick side talk about sharp, actual, <u>physical</u> pain...

Ice it. Ten minutes on, ten minutes off. Repeat. NEVER use heat of any kind, including hot water, unless it is only dull pain or the pain is gone. Heat may make your pain feel better for a while, but it actually exacerbates the problem by increasing inflammation.

Use this acronym: RICE

Rest
Ice
Compression
Elevation

Try Traumeel, too, which is a homeopathic, anti-inflam-matory topical cream or gel that helps relieve sore and damaged muscles. Traumeel is from Germany, and it is made up of fourteen different botanical ingredients, as well as several different minerals that work together to create amazing healing power. It's a great idea to always have a tube in your medicine cabinet for whenever needed. Traumeel can be found at most health food stores. Be well!

WISDOM SNACK #28 - GIVING

"If you wish to experience peace,
provide peace for another."
- Tenzin Gyatso

KNOW that one of the healthiest things you can do in life is give from love to another being... whether that being is human, animal, or plant.

When you have what I like to call a "heartpull" to give to and nurture another, there is something divine that happens through you. It's called PURE LOVE.

Giving from love is more powerful than you think.

When you give out of obligation, or from fear, or from guilt, yes, it is still giving, but not in the sense I am referring to here.

Giving from love is heart-based, not brain-based. When you give from your heart, you are touching the essence of life in a way like nothing else can.

This type of giving comes easily, freely, and without need for recognition or response. It is simply a release of pure love out into the world... and you already KNOW that what you give out comes back to you.

As you help others from pure love, you will feel pure love. You will feel peace. You will feel joy.

We are all here to help each other. That means others help YOU when you need it, too. Don't take away their joy!

Your giving from love may be giving of money. In today's world, money is needed by so many, and this is a very beautiful gift. Money, as we already KNOW, is not the "root of all evil." It is merely energy that helps us do what we need to do.

Until our economy is based on a higher form of trans-action, money is a lovely and highly appreciated way to give.

Your giving from love may be giving of time and exper-tise... to a child, to an animal shelter, to a struggling new business owner, etc. Whatever it is, recognize that your gifts are valuable, and deserve to be shared with others.

Your giving of love may simply be sending prayer, or energy, or love silently to another who is suffering. Just connecting with another in a heartspace during your busy day is a gift.

No matter how much or how little you have or choose to give, it will ALL be appreciated.

Giving from love is one of the biggest healers for de-pression. Depression is a self-focused DIS-ease, and it is so easy to spiral downward as we stay focused on our own losses, sadness, and despair.

Giving to another restores our connection to life, brings fulfillment and joy, and helps us find purpose in living.

Choose life. Do a random act of kindness for another today. KNOW how it feels to give freely, without expectation of return or reward.

To your loving, giving heart!

♥♥♥ *Kathy*

WISDOM SNACK #29 - SLEEP

"To sleep, perchance to dream - ay, there's the rub."
- William Shakespeare

Having trouble sleeping lately? You are not alone. At least 40 million Americans each year suffer from chronic, long-term sleep disorders, and an additional 20 million experience occasional sleep disturbances.

Then we all go out and drive, work, make important decisions... yikes!

A good night's sleep:

✦ lowers stress

✦ lessens depression

+ improves memory

+ curbs inflammation

+ spurs creativity

+ improves athletic performance

+ lessens ADHD in children

+ assists weight loss

+ helps prevent heart disease and diabetes

+ helps avoid accidents

+ improves grades

+ gives greater emotional balance

+ helps one live longer

Here are some great tips to KNOW to help you fall asleep and stay asleep:

1. Keep the lights low in the bedroom. Bright lights say "Daytime!" If you read in bed, read in the lowest comfortable light.
2. Choose non-energy boosting foods and drinks after lunch.
3. Yes, take a warm bath, but not right before bed. Your body needs time to cool down to reach deep slumber.

4. Make your bedroom a calm sanctuary, with soothing colors. Use your bed only for sleep, reading, and sex.

5. Do not have a TV, cell phone, iPad, laptop, or anything else emitting EMFs (electric and magnetic fields) in your bedroom.

6. The light from the devices in #5 above actually stimulates the brain... so try not to use any of these devices for at least two hours before getting into bed.

7. Ideally, drink no alcohol at all. If you do, always drink pure water before and after each glass, definitely no alcohol after dinner, and always in moderation. Alcohol decreases deep sleep and increases arousals from sleep.

8. For extra help, try Bach Flower™"Rescue Sleep" or Hyland's "Calms Forte." Both are homeopathic, non-toxic, non-addictive, have no side effects, are all-natural, and may be found at most health food stores.

9. Receive regular massage. Studies have shown that people receiving massages on a regular basis experience less pain, less depression, less anxiety, and fewer sleep disturbances than even those using relaxation therapy. A one hour massage from a qualified therapist is said to have the same restorative value as four hours of sleep in bed. A one

and one-half hour massage has the same restorative value as six hours of sleep in bed... and so
on. Massage helps every single system of the body.
It is not a luxury - it is a sound, preventative, and
restorative form of health care.

"A ruffled mind makes a restless pillow."
- Charlotte Brontë

Try this restful "Reclined Butterfly" pose from Tanya
Boulton, managing teacher at Pure Yoga East in New
York City:

Lie on your back with the soles of your feet together
and your knees bent and dropping toward the floor.
Place your arms, palms up, by your sides, keeping your
shoulders back and your chest open. Close your eyes
and inhale through your nose while slowly counting to
four, then exhale while counting back down to one.
Continue for ten minutes, or as long as it takes you to
feel fully relaxed.

POWER NAPPING -
FAR BETTER FOR YOU THAN COFFEE!

Researchers have found in recent years that the human
body requires only as much sleep as the brain will allow

it. In other words, so long as the brain is functioning at full capacity, there's no great requirement for sleep. The big thing is that the brain may need a rest every now and then during the day. Apparently, the brain can refresh itself and go on "like with a full tank of gas" with just a short, 20-minute power nap. There is a fantastic article online called "The Secret (and Surprising) Power of Naps" by Jennifer Soong at www.webmd.com. Try to make the time to go there and read it.

Make sleep, and power napping, a priority in your life, and watch your life improve. Oh, and get a great 100% organic mattress, too. We spend one third of our lives in bed. Make it healthy, hypoallergenic, eco-friendly, and blissful.

Sweet dreams to your refreshed, renewed, relaxed, re-energized self!

♥♥♥ Kathy

WISDOM SNACK #30 - LOVE

"Love cures people -
both the ones who give it
and the ones who receive it."
- Karl Menninger

There was no other way to end our thirty days together than what unites us all... LOVE.

No matter what has happened in your life... no matter how broken, or disillusioned, or frustrated, or sad times in your life may have been, LOVE has always been there and available to heal you.

Everything, when you boil it down to its purest essence, stems from either love or fear.

As you have already learned in this program, fear-based decisions, actions, and behaviors ultimately hurt everyone, especially the one coming from fear. (Fear weakens the kidneys in physical manifestation, and plays havoc with the mind and spirit.) Fear is usually the ego-mind running you, and it walks hand-in-hand with stress.

Pure love-based decisions, actions, and behaviors are the only way to peace. They come from the heart, and heal in ways that can seem miraculous.

Imagine a world where everyone operates based on LOVE. I imagine it all the time.

Fear is simply insecurity made manifest.

Although LOVE cannot be scientifically proven, all scientists agree it exists. All human beings agree it exists.

It is the starting point. It is the ending point. If we allow it, it is also everything in between.

If you do not give yourself completely over to love, the previous 29 lessons in this program can't fully do what they are meant to do.

Love is the ultimate answer, the ultimate key to life. Without it, there will always be locked doors in your way.

BE love.

Love everything. Love everyone. Love your partner, your dog, and your washing machine. Love the tree in your back yard. Love your neighbor down the street. Love your body. Love your mind. Love your spirit. Love the bird singing outside your window. Love our Earth. Love everything you see, hear, smell, feel, and touch. Love what is, what has been, and what can be.

Keep doing THAT... every minute of every day. No matter what.

Watch miracles happen.

You are not alone. You are divine. You are perfect, exactly as you are.

KNOW you are loved.

I love you.

Be well always and in all ways, and I thank you profoundly for taking this journey with me. Please share it with whomever you think may benefit. Together, we will change the world.

In Health, With Love and Gratitude,

♥♥♥

CONGRATULATIONS, WISDOM SEEKER!

You did it! Awesome! How do you feel?! Remember, you have just taken in a LOT of information, so take baby steps, and do the pieces that feel right for you now.

Continue to do more and more of the suggestions as you can, and notice the shifts that begin taking place in your life. It's all GOOD!

Thank you for sharing your time with me, and for being open to possibilities for greater health and healing.

I love you, and I honor the "(K)NEW" you! ☺

 ♥♥♥

P.S. If you would like to continue growing with The Power of Know, please join me on my Facebook page at www. facebook.com/powerofknow. Thanks, and see you online!

GRATITUDE

I AM grateful to all who have loved me along my winding path... those who have lifted me up, supported my dreams, made me laugh, taught me needed wisdom, inspired new ideas, provided light when there was darkness, and helped me heal from the inside out. Thanks to <u>you</u>, I am still here, doing whatever I can to help others, and finally living life in a more peaceful, simpler, less-stressed, healthier, and happier way.

I AM also grateful to those along the way who were not kind to me. While not condoning your behaviors, thanks to <u>you</u>, I know I can help others experiencing similar life journeys. Thanks to <u>you</u>, I can empathize whole-heartedly with those who are afraid to be who they really are, those who suffer behind closed doors, those who wonder if life is worth it. Thanks to <u>you</u>, I eventually learned the gift of forgiveness, and became a vessel of love, embracing everyone.

I AM grateful for the education and wisdom from truth-seekers like my Naturopath Jim Reese, and all the myriad friends, teachers, clients, authors, public figures, and family members who continue to teach me every day about being authentic and coming from love no matter what.

I AM grateful to YOU, dear reader, for joining me on this journey of life in healthy, all-natural, loving, and kind ways.

Last, but certainly not least, I AM grateful to two very special men whom I first met as a young girl at Moravian College in Bethlehem, Pennsylvania - Jon Van Valkenburg and Vince Pantalone. Thanks to them, my belief in miracles and the value of always following your heart was proven beyond a shadow of a doubt.

I AM profoundly grateful.

Love, Health, and Peace to all,

 ♥♥♥

ABOUT THE AUTHOR

Holistic Wellness Educator and Coach, Nationally Certified Massage Therapist and Instructor, and Level I Bach Flower™ Practitioner, Kathy Ozzard Chism lives her life to help heal others and lift the world to a higher vibration.

She loves to watch the positive shifts that occur when people use her suggested all-natural methods and ideas to improve their lives, and supports all who come to her for help with LOVE.

Kathy has always believed that if you are given a dream, you are also given the ability to somehow make it come true... and she has dreamed a LOT into her life.

Along with the above, she has held careers as varied as Fourth Grade Teacher, Flight Attendant, Licensed Interior Architect and Designer, Sales Manager, National Meeting Planner, Calligrapher, Actress, Model, Voiceover Artist, Writer, Proofreader/Editor, and Global Nonprofit Founder and Director.

A world traveler and lover of education, Kathy holds a B.A. degree from Moravian College, Bethlehem, PA, an A.A. degree from International Fine Arts College, Miami, FL, and helped create an A.S. degree program for Massage Therapy in Rohnert Park, CA. She earned her private pilot's license while living in the Bahamas, and has lived in New Jersey, Pennsylvania, Virginia, Illinois, Florida, California, Texas, and New York as well.

A vegetarian (now mostly vegan) since age 16, she has always lived in a health-conscious and caring way, seeking all-natural, organic, and homeopathic ways for healing.

Then in early 2009, Kathy nearly died from stress and "doing too much." It was a major turning point.

"The Power of Know" is the result, with Kathy's journey back to life now helping to heal others in a deeper way than before. She focuses on assisting her clients with simplifying their lives, letting go of negative emotions, and choosing a wide variety of all-natural ways to heal mind, body, and spirit.

Her first book, "Garage Sale Success Secrets," teaches all the steps for de-cluttering and creating very successful garage sales... with a number of Zen-like tidbits for living a simpler, less stressful, more joyful life sprinkled throughout its pages.

To learn more about Kathy, please visit
www.kathychism.com.

66243096R00111

Made in the USA
Charleston, SC
15 January 2017